Arthur S. Link
Princeton University
General Editor for History

Donated from

the personal

library of

Dr. Meredith C.

Haines

The AHM American History Series
under the series editorship of
John Hope Franklin, University of Chicago
Abraham S. Eisenstadt, Brooklyn College

Cover photo: The Bettmann Archive

E
165
B28

Irving H. Bartlett
CARNEGIE-MELLON UNIVERSITY

The American Mind in the Mid-Nineteenth Century

AHM Publishing Corporation
Northbrook, Illinois 60062

HIEBERT LIBRARY
Fresno Pacific College - M. B. Seminary
Fresno, Calif. 93702
WITHDRAWN
48898

Copyright © 1967

AHM PUBLISHING CORPORATION

All rights reserved.

This book, or parts thereof, must not be used
or reproduced in any manner without written
permission. For information address the
publisher, AHM PUBLISHING CORPO-
RATION, 3110 North Arlington Heights
Road, Arlington Heights, Illinois 60004.

ISBN: 0-88295-701-5
(Formerly 0-690-07414X)

Library of Congress Card Number: 67-14299

PRINTED IN THE UNITED STATES OF AMERICA
778
Ninth Printing

EDITORS' FOREWORD

It is a commonplace that each age writes its own history, for the reason that man sees the past in the foreshortened perspective of his own experience. This has certainly been true of the writing of American history. The purpose of our historical writing remains constant: to offer us a more certain sense of where we are going by indicating the road we have taken in getting there. But it is precisely because our own generation is redefining its direction, the way other generations have redefined theirs before us, that the substance of our historical writing is changing. We are thinking anew of our direction because of our newer values and premises, our newer sense of how we can best fulfill the goals of our society, our newer outlook on the meaning of American life. Thus, the vitality of the present inspires the vitality of our writing about the past.

It is the plan of the *AHM American History Series* to offer the reader a survey of the point of arrival of recent scholarship on the central themes and problems of American history. The scholars we have invited to do the respective volumes of the series are younger individuals whose monographs have been well received by their peers and who have demonstrated their mastery of the subjects on which they are writing. The author of each volume has undertaken to present a summation of the principal lines of discussion that historians of a particular subject have been pursuing. However, he has not written a mere digest of historical literature. The author has been concerned, moreover, to offer the reader a sufficient factual and narrative account to help him perceive the larger dimensions of the subject. Each author, moreover, has arrived at his own conclusions about those aspects of his subject that have been matters of difference and controversy. In effect, he has written not only

v

about where the subject stands in historiography but also about where he himself stands on the subject. And each volume concludes with an extensive critical essay on authorities.

The books in this series are designed for use in the basic course in American history, although they could be used, with great benefit, in advanced courses as well. Such a series has a particular utility in times such as these, when the traditional format of our American history courses is being altered to accommodate a greater diversity of texts and reading materials. The series offers a number of distinct advantages. It extends and deepens the dimensions of course work in American history. In proceeding beyond the confines of the traditional textbook, it makes clear that the study of our past is, more than the student might otherwise infer, at once complex, sophisticated, and profound. It presents American history as a subject of continuing vitality and fresh investigation. The work of experts in their respective fields, it opens up to the student the rich findings of historical inquiry. It invites the student to join with his older and more experienced colleagues in pondering anew the major themes and problems of our past. It challenges the student to participate actively in exploring American history and to seek out its wider reaches on his own.

John Hope Franklin
Abraham S. Eisenstadt

CONTENTS

ONE

Interpreting American Democratic Thought

The American mind from about 1830 to 1860 is both a product of and a commentator upon the expanding political, social, and economic democracy of the period. Three themes that we will find recurring often in the thought of the period are closely related to those discussed by Ralph Gabriel in *The Course of American Democratic Thought*. They are (1) belief in the free individual (which implies equality), (2) belief in the moral law (which implies religion), and (3) belief in the American mission (which implies nationalism). A fourth theme, requiring more explanation, may be described as the ambivalent response in the American mind to the pace of change. Whether measured in terms of population increase, territorial expansion, urbanization, economic growth, or technological development, American society was being transformed during this period at a spectacular rate. Some Americans, like Whitman, rejoiced in the change. Others, like Hawthorne and Melville, were skeptical. A few, like Calhoun, despaired. The most characteristic response, as William Taylor points out in a recent study entitled *Cavalier and Yankee,* was an ambivalent one: "The rapidity with which every aspect of national life was changing produced both sets of response: The optimism and the despair. Some of the alarm appears to have sprung from the very fact that American institutions were free and men were free to change them—for better or for worse. It was precisely because the Union had grown and changed so rapidly, for example, that people began to wonder whether it could survive."

For a long time the interpretation of American thought during the middle of the nineteenth century was dominated by the work of Frederick Jackson Turner and Vernon Parrington. Turner held that American democratic ideals and aspirations were a product of the frontier, and Parrington described the development of American thought during the period as an ideological conflict in which liberals in the Jefferson-Jackson tradition attempted to defend democratic values against attack from a declining Federalist aristocracy and a rising, acquisitive capitalistic oligarchy.

Both of these interpretations must be modified in the light of recent scholarship. Turner's frontier thesis has been attacked for both substantive and methodological reasons. In a recent book entitled *The Frontier Mind,* Arthur Moore takes issue with the assumption that the West was the custodian of American virtue and vigor. Taking Kentucky as a case Moore finds the typical frontiersman to have been a cultural barbarian characterized by sloth, rapacity, and violence, ignorant of the intellectual inheritance of the Enlightenment and, except for his ability to kill Indians and survive in the wilderness, unable to contribute greatly to the realization of the American dream. A more fundamental objection to the Turner Thesis is made in terms of methodology. Many scholars have pointed out that if the frontier has been the decisive influence in shaping American civilization, other nations with frontiers should have shaped similar civilizations. It is easy to show that this has not been true, and thus modern historians look for other explanations.

Parrington's interpretation of American thought as a fierce domestic dialogue pitting liberals and radicals against conservatives and reactionaries must also be modified. Louis Hartz's *The Liberal Tradition in America* offers a challenging counter-interpretation. Hartz finds the key to his thesis in Tocqueville's statement that Americans were born free. Lacking a feudal tradition they did not have to develop an authentic radical tradition. A liberal tradition (Hartz calls this "The Lockian ethos") arose in America, "and this is the factor which like some ultimate Hegelian force keeps showing its face in the various aspects" of our history. Almost without exception, Hartz argues, American thinkers have agreed with each other in accepting the Lockian ethos (the right of private property and the right of self-government). According to Hartz any society developing as America did in the first half of the nineteenth century, with no feudal background, no peasantry, and no proletariat, was bound to move toward democracy and capitalism. "The irony of early American history, however, is that these impulses, instead of supplementing each other, seemed to fight a tremendous political battle." Jacksonian Democrats likened the Whigs to the corrupt Old World aristocracy; the Whigs rejoined by comparing the Jacksonians to the bloodthirsty rabble in Europe. Yet both had immeasurably more in common with each other than with their alleged counterparts abroad. The typical American thinker invariably represented the American liberal consensus. Parrington's mistake was in confusing the rhetorical differences of political opponents with nonexistent ideological differences.

As we pursue our examination of the American mind in the middle of the nineteenth century we can expect to find repeated emphasis placed on the values of individualism and equality, the moral law and religion, the American mission and nationalism, the ambivalent response to change. We will trace the development of American thought in a burgeoning democratic society, searching both for the liberal consensus which joined America's most significant thinkers together and for the significant differences which divided them.

TWO

Religion, Philosophy, and Science in the American Democracy

Through religion, philosophy, and science men attempt to understand and bring themselves into harmonious relationship with the universe. In our own time philosophy and science have become highly specialized disciplines and have lost their intimate connection with religious inquiry. In the three decades before the Civil War, however, they were inseparable. Theologians, philosophers, and scientists, whatever their special interests, shared and expressed the common values of American democracy.

RELIGION

In 1922 Harold Stearns edited an influential book entitled *Civilization in the United States.* He included over thirty articles on subjects ranging all the way from politics and science to sex and humor, but he left out any discussion of religion in America. The reason he gave was simple. He could not find anyone to write on the subject. Two years ago a distinguished American historian, Henry F. May, contended in the *American Historical Review* that "for the study and understanding of American culture, the recovery of American religious history may well be the most important achievement of the last thirty years."

The renewal of interest in the history of American religion can be explained in different ways. It is partly a result of the enormous impact that theologians like Reinhold Niebuhr have had on American intellectuals in the last thirty years. It derives somewhat from the work of American literary critics like F. O. Matthiessen, which has become increasingly concerned with the religious ideas of such classic American writers as Hawthorne and Melville. In American historiography it is due above all to the scholarship of Perry Miller. In the foreword to his first book, *Orthodoxy in Massachusetts,* published in 1933, Miller justified his exhaustive attention to religious ideas by venturing the thesis "that whatever may be the case in other centuries, in the sixteenth and seventeenth certain men of decisive importance took religion seriously; that they often followed spiritual dictates in comparative disregard of ulterior considerations; that those who led the Great Migration to Massachusetts and who founded the colony were predominantly men of this stamp." Although Miller was primarily concerned with the intellectual history of New England during the colonial period, his prodigious scholarship ranged freely into later periods, and he demonstrated that theology was a primary concern of the American mind at least through the middle of the nineteenth century.

Tocqueville emphasized the pre-eminence of religion to Americans in the middle of the nineteenth century when he claimed that there was "no country in the world in which Christianity retained a greater influence over the souls of men." Our agreement with Tocqueville, however, does not mean that the religious temper of the country in the 1830's, 40's, and 50's was simply a further flowering of seeds planted by the Puritans. Perhaps the ghost of Jonathan Edwards was still abroad in the land, but every year it grew more wraithlike and lost more of its haunting power. The men and women who flocked to support Jackson's banner were the grandchildren and great-grandchildren of Edwards's auditors. Many of them still had an appetite for strong religion, but they wanted it on terms befitting a free-born people who had rejected the tyrannies of the Old World for the democracy of the New. Calvin's famous five points which emphasized the sovereignty of God and the depravity and helplessness of man needed to be rewritten. Since the high office of the theologian is not to destroy but to sustain and increase the faith of his fathers, it is not surprising to find that the most representative religious thinkers of the period, however they might disagree over specific points, found common ground in their attempt to make religious faith palatable to a generation brought up in the democratic faith—a faith that emphasized the rights and dignity of man and the self-improvement of mankind.

The history of religious thought during this period is essentially the history of the transformation of Calvinism, and its immediate roots go back to the eighteenth century when such splendid representatives of the American Enlightenment as Benjamin Franklin and Jonathan Edwards were in their prime. These two men, in some ways so different, were of one mind in their concern to make their religious ideas conform to the demands of rational men and to the discoveries of modern science. Although born into a strongly Calvinistic family, Franklin was repelled by the harsh strictures of Calvinism. When he was about fifteen, a time when most pious young men were expected to worry over the state of their souls, Franklin discovered deism. The religious ideas which he developed with the help of his reading in Locke, Newton, and other Enlightenment writers left little room for supernaturalism. Calvin's God of wrath was transformed into a benevolent master mechanic and prime mover of the universe. The quest for salvation was replaced by the quest for morality and worldly success, and the sense of sin gave way to the knowledge that man by the use of reason could live blamelessly without God's intervention.

Like Franklin, Jonathan Edwards also studied the works of Locke and Newton, but his brilliant treatises were essentially a work of conservation, and had the effect of strengthening Calvinist orthodoxy by showing how modern refinements in psychology and physics supported the doctrines of natural depravity, predestination, and supernatural grace. Franklin believed that morality was the core of religious life and that the world would reward the moral man. Edwards insisted that man was a naturally sinful creature, utterly beyond redemption unless God chose to infuse truly religious affections into him in the form of a genuine "saving" or "gracious" experience.

During Edwards's own lifetime the great majority of American believers were more sympathetic to Calvinism than to the liberal ideas of Franklin. By the turn of the century, however, the Calvinists had turned to the defensive almost everywhere, and for the next several decades the common mission of our most significant Protestant theologians was to justify religion in doctrinal terms that the new generations would accept. William Ellery Channing attempted to do this by emphasizing the liberalism of Unitarian Christianity. Charles Grandison Finney attempted to do it by preaching a new kind of revivalism. Horace Bushnell sought to do it by recasting the whole structure of orthodox theology according to the temper of the new age.

William Ellery Channing

It is difficult for modern readers to appreciate the impact of William Ellery Channing on the generation that came into maturity in the pre-Civil War period. When Channing died in 1842, Theodore Parker claimed that "no man in America" had left such a sphere of influence, "no man since Washington" had "done so much to elevate his country."

Channing was born in Newport, Rhode Island, in 1780. He graduated from Harvard in 1798 and returned there three years later to pursue theological studies. In 1803 he assumed the ministry of Boston's Federal Street Congregation. He retained this pulpit throughout his career and from it preached most of the sermons that established his reputation as the father of American Unitarianism.

Channing is the supreme example in American thought of the Enlightenment mind reaching out for romanticism. He was literally a child of the American Revolution. His grandfather had signed the Declaration of Independence. His father had studied with James Madison at Princeton, and as a boy of seven Channing himself had been present at the convention when Rhode Island ratified the Constitution. He grew up with the new nation, and the optimistic view of human nature on which the American experiment was based greatly influenced his own thinking.

Neither Edwards nor Franklin offered spiritual nourishment for Channing. Edwards's Calvinism was too severe, and the barren history of New England theology after Edwards, composed for the most part of a seemingly endless succession of wrangling controversies over the precise definition of narrow theological concepts, was distasteful to Channing. Franklin's deism, on the other hand, was too cold and much too secular. Channing did not share Franklin's worldliness. Like Edwards he had gone through his own solitary vigil of the spirit and he could never subscribe to a religious system which substituted a first cause for a personal God.

Channing's course lay somewhere between the extremes of Edwards and Franklin. It was preceded by the development of a group of liberal Congregational ministers clustered mostly around Boston about the time of the Great Awakening. These clergymen, of whom Charles Chauncy (1704-1787) was probably the most influential, rejected predestination, and without questioning the authority of Scripture or the existence of a personal God, emphasized the rational character of God and man. Channing represents the culmination of this aspect of the Enlightenment.

Although he was not a systematic theologian, Channing based all of his writing on two fundamental assumptions. The first is the belief in the dignity of man as a rational creature. "Say what we may," Channing wrote in one of his most famous sermons, "God has given us a rational nature and will call us to account for it." God had seen fit to communicate with men through the Bible in human language, and Channing expected them to study it as they would any other book, by applying their rational faculties to it. "We reason about the Bible," he asserted, "precisely as civilians do about the Constitution under which we live."

Channing's second basic assumption was that God is not a sovereign power (as Edwards had insisted) but a morally perfect being. "It is not because his will is irresistible, but because his will is the perfection of virtue, that we pay him allegiance. We cannot bow before a being however great who governs tyrannically."

Armed with these two convictions Channing led the liberals in their attempt to dismantle Calvinism. They attacked the doctrine of the Trinity on the grounds that a God conceived of as both three and one was unintelligible and unscriptural. Because they insisted on upholding the unity of God, Channing and his supporters were called Unitarians. The debate over the Trinity, however, was far less damaging to the orthodox cause than "The Moral Argument Against Calvinism." Channing gave this title to an article which he published in 1820 specifically attacking "the five thorny points of Calvinism" for "degrading man and God":

> Calvinism owes its perpetuity to the influence of fear in palsying the moral nature. Men's minds and consciences are subdued by terror so that they dare not confess, even to themselves, the shrinking which they feel from the unworthy views which this system gives of God, and, by thus smothering their just abhorrence, they gradually extinguish it, and even come to vindicate in God what would disgrace his creatures.

Many New England Calvinists still believed that Jonathan Edwards in his treatise on free will had demonstrated that man had no power, without a supernatural visitation from God, to improve his moral condition. Edwards had made a famous distinction between the natural and moral inability in man, and lesser theologians had been chewing over the distinction ever since. Channing dismissed the entire issue as unworthy of serious discussion. "Common people cannot understand this distinction, cannot split this hair," he wrote, "and it is no small objection to Calvinism that, according to its ablest defenders, it can only be reconciled to God's perfections by a metaphysical subtility which the mass of people cannot comprehend."

Thus did Channing dispose of Edwards and the great theological system that thinker had so splendidly reinforced. Edwards's surely was the greater mind, but in appealing to the common sense of ordinary people Channing spoke for the coming age. In just eight years Andrew Jackson would be President, and in his first message to the Congress he would argue for the principle of rotation in office on the grounds that "the duties of all public officers are, or at least admit of being made, so plain and simple that men of intelligence may readily qualify themselves for their performance."

Channing was never a Jackson man. Neither was he a transcendentalist, believing as he did in the authority of Scripture and the reality of miracles. And yet, in some of his most eloquent sermons, when Channing emphasized man's "likeness to God" and the "traces of infinity in the human mind," his readers and listeners might well have wondered if he did not mean to identify human dignity with divinity. Certainly his influence on Emerson and Theodore Parker was profound. Emerson dated the beginning of New England's renaissance about 1820 (one year after Channing's famous "Unitarian Christianity" sermon), and said "we could not then spare a single word he uttered in public, not so much the reading lesson in Scripture, or a hymn. . . . A poor little invalid all his life, he is yet one of those who vindicate the power of the American race to produce greatness."

William Ellery Channing did not convert America to

Unitarianism. That denomination remained small in numbers throughout the pre-Civil War period. His influence, however, went far beyond his own denomination, and his significance in our intellectual history lies in his attempt to synthesize the diverse strands of thought in America which appeared in his own lifetime, and thus build a bridge from the Enlightenment to the democracy of mid-nineteenth century America.

Charles Grandison Finney

There were two great periods of religious revival in America before the Civil War. The first, which we associate with the name of Jonathan Edwards, lasted from 1734 to 1756. The second lasted from 1795 to 1835 and is associated with the name of Charles Grandison Finney. Contrasting Finney's attitude toward religious revivals with Edwards's tells us much about the religious mind in America in the second quarter of the nineteenth century.

The second Great Awakening began on the frontier, flaming up in a series of Great Camp Meetings in Kentucky and Tennessee in 1795. The preachers who tended the fires, Methodists, Baptists, and Presbyterians for the most part, were roughhewn, uneducated, and far more interested in saving souls than in preaching a consistent Calvinism. They believed that preaching that emphasized the complete and utter inability of sinners to do anything to improve their condition hindered revivals, and they sought a theology to sustain the great wave of religious excitement generated on the frontier. Charles Grandison Finney provided that theology.

Finney, who was born in 1792, started his career as a lawyer, but after his conversion left the law to take up a career in evangelism which ultimately took him to a highly successful ministry in New York's Broadway Tabernacle and to the presidency of Oberlin College. In his prime Finney was probably the most powerful preacher in America. The religious enthusiasm that swept through upstate New York like wildfire in the 1820's and 30's was largely his work. By the time of his death in 1875 he had been the dean of American revivalists for almost half a century.

Finney's *Lectures on Revivals* (1835) is intended both as a handbook on the conduct of revivals and a statement of theology. Consequently it has a strong practical flavor and is closely related to his personal experience. After his conversion, when Finney decided to study religious doctrine seriously, he found he had "nowhere to go but directly to the Bible and the philosophy or workings" of his own mind. This statement is similar to what William Ellery Channing had said in his famous sermon "Unitarian Christianity" seventeen years earlier. Finney was not influenced by Channing, but his religious ideas blend evangelical fervor with the kind of rational approach to religion which Channing had made famous. His theology is based on the assumption that God, being benevolent and reasonable, does not demand of men more than they can perform. Finney believed that every man was able "to repent, to believe in Christ and to accept salvation." He likened the sinner to a man in a trance approaching a precipice. A stranger appears on the scene in time to shout a warning. The man turns, quivering and aghast, "from the verge of death." Thus does the preacher "awaken" the sinner. Once awakened it is up to the sinner, stirred on by ministerial exhortations, to repent and accept the divine blessing. Once saved the Christian was expected to vigorously apply Christian principles to the affairs of this world. To this extent, as we will see in the next chapter, Finney's preaching and theology had a direct impact on the reform impulse in America.

Finney looked both to the future and to the past, and it would be a serious mistake not to recognize that he had much closer ties to the old orthodoxy than did a liberal like Channing. Finney, like most Americans at this time, believed in a personal God and a personal Devil. He believed in the reality of Hell and the justice of a God intent on meting out eternal punishment to the unconverted. In these points he agreed with Jonathan Edwards. As William McLoughlin points out, however, in his study *Modern Revivalism: Charles Grandison Finney to Billy Graham,* Finney was essentially modern in his approach to revivals. When Edwards wrote to a friend describing the results of the Great Awakening in 1735, he had concluded by saying, "to God be all the Glory whose work alone it is." A century later Finney described a revival as "not a miracle or dependent on a miracle in any sense. It is a purely philosophical result of the right use of constituted means." By "philosophical" Finney meant scientific. His preacher was both a man of faith and a scientist—a rainmaker who would no longer be content to sit docilely in a parched country when he knew how to prompt the heavenly showers himself. The revivalist in the age of Jackson was an optimist, at home in a world which he understood and labored increasingly to perfect.

Horace Bushnell

During the same year that Finney published his *Lectures on Revivals,* Horace Bushnell, then in the second year of his pastorate in Hartford, Connecticut, was lamenting the over-emphasis on revivalism which had reduced his role to that of "a church clock for beating time and marking the years, while the effective ministry of the word was to be dispersed by a class of professed revivalists." Religion was being sought almost exclusively in the explosive outbreak which prostrated the faithful at the camp meeting. "It could not be conceived," Bushnell complained, "how any one might be in the Spirit and maintain a constancy of growth, in the calmer and more private methods of duty, patience and fidelity on the level of ordinary life."

Bushnell, the first really creative theologian in America after Jonathan Edwards, was born in Litchfield County, Connecticut, in 1802. He studied theology at Yale, where he read the works of Scottish common-sense philosophers like Dugald Stewart, and studied under Nathaniel W. Taylor, then busily at work developing a theology which modified the Edwardian system by providing for free will. His real teacher, however, was Coleridge.

James Marsh, president of the University of Vermont, introduced Coleridge to the American public by editing *Aids to Reflection* in 1829. The rapturous reception to this book, especially in Boston, Cambridge, and Concord, is a landmark in American intellectual history. It marks the point at which

America's most creative minds turned away from the English and Scottish philosophy of the eighteenth century to refresh themselves at the springs of transcendentalism. It is important to understand, however, that Emerson, Margaret Fuller, and Theodore Parker were not the only ones to read Coleridge. As a divinity student in the embattled fortress of orthodoxy at Yale, Bushnell probably read *Aids to Reflection* for the first time in 1831. Coleridge, and later the German theologian Schleiermacher, and Victor Cousin, the French popularizer of German philosophy, became for Bushnell what Locke and Newton had been for Jonathan Edwards. They provided him with the intellectual tools necessary to reshape orthodox Protestant theology according to the spirit of a new age.

Bushnell's three most important books are *Christian Nurture* (1847), *God in Christ* (1849), and *Nature and the Supernatural* (1859). In *Christian Nurture* Bushnell struck out at the emphasis on revivalism that had harried him at the beginning of his ministry. He denied the doctrine that every child was born sinful and could not become a Christian without the transforming emotional experience of conversion. The revolutionary thesis of Bushnell's book was stated in one sentence: "The child is to grow up a Christian and never know himself as being otherwise." In rejecting a "piety of conquest" for a piety of love, Bushnell argued that every family was an organic unit and that the spirit of God passed naturally from pious parents to their children.

In maintaining the organic unity of the family, I mean to assert that a power is exerted by parents over children not only when they teach, encourage, persuade and govern, but without any purposed control whatever, the bond is so intimate that they do it unconsciously and undesignedly—they must do it. Their character, feelings, spirits and principles must propagate themselves, whether they will or not.

The kingdom of evil is sustained through the operation of the same organic laws. A child nurtured on the bosom of a sinful family will naturally become a sinner, not because he is born of sinful seed, but because his character will have been steeped in an atmosphere of evil. Since it is unthinkable to assume that God could have ordained organic laws solely as a vehicle for depravity, Bushnell claims that the great task for Christians is to employ the organic unity of the family as an instrument of grace.

Bushnell's debt to Coleridge is most clearly shown in his volume *God in Christ,* which he introduces with an important essay on language. Words are rooted in nature. There is an external and an internal language. The former, concerned solely with natural objects and actions, Bushnell terms a "noun language." The latter, involving communication of thought, is possible "only as there is a Logos in the outward world, answering to the Logos or internal reason" of man. Since spiritual ideas can be expressed only through natural symbols, or words, it follows that the word representing the idea is always something less than the idea itself and can never be used to fashion a system of dogmatic truth. The limitations of logic as a vehicle for spiritual truth are thus shown to be obvious. Such truth is best expressed, not through definitions and syllogisms, but metaphorically. Since all words are imprecise, "language will be ever trying to mend its own deficiencies by multiplying its forms of representation."

Bushnell describes revealed Christianity as "God's coming into expression through histories and rites, through an incarnation and through language." In *Christian Nurture* he had contended that religious truth is an organic force in human life. Now he insists that language also is organic. The function of words is vital, not mechanical. When men recognize the insufficiency of words to demonstrate spiritual truth they may finally be brought to experience it.

> We shall receive the truth of God in a more entire organic and organific manner, as being itself essentially vital power. It will not be our endeavor to pull the truth into analytic distinctions, as if theology were a kind of inorganic chemistry, . . . but we shall delight in truth more as a concrete, vital nature, incarnated in all fact and symbol around us.

Using this as his intellectual base it is easy for Bushnell to show that controversial doctrines like the Trinity and the

Atonement can never be explained in a literal sense, but should be understood as God's way of expressing himself to man through language (the Bible), and thus necessarily through metaphor and symbol.

Like many creative thinkers Bushnell was not really understood in his own time. The Calvinists in Connecticut accused him of heresy, and the liberals around Boston tried to claim him as their own. Bushnell, himself, apparently felt his mission to be "a reproduction of orthodoxy from the standpoint of Unitarianism." By this he meant a reconciliation of Channing's humanism with the Christ-centered theology of Calvinism. Modern scholars frequently refer to Bushnell as one who "transcendentalized" Calvinism, but this judgment needs to be qualified. Despite his belief in the spiritual nature of man, Bushnell insisted on the reality of sin and the necessity for saving grace dispensed supernaturally through the office of revealed Christianity. Although he avowed the immanence of God in nature, he was careful not to identify God with nature. The sense of a personal God, apart from nature and towering above it (*Nature and the Supernatural,* 1859), was always present in his thinking.

Horace Bushnell was a much more complex thinker than either Channing or Finney, and it is more difficult to know where to place him among his contemporaries. To the extent that he denied the conception of natural depravity and the necessity for a supernaturally launched conversion experience, he was responding to the new liberalism. To the extent that he advocated a view of natural laws through which God appeared to man not as master mechanic but as presence, he was responding to the influence of writers like Coleridge who were also decisive in helping to shape American transcendentalism. Bushnell also represented the American mind at mid-century by his ambivalent attitude toward change. In her recent biography, *Horace Bushnell: Minister to a Changing America,* Barbara Cross finds her main theme in the tension created by Bushnell's attempt to accommodate "Christianity to the contemporary imagination" without being false to the tradition that he served. In an age of intense individualism and innovation Bushnell refused to let

go of the past. Above all he sought to reinterpret and thus conserve the great doctrines of the Reformation which had been
so close to the hearts of his Puritan ancestors.

PHILOSOPHY

The American mind before the Civil War did not produce a
systematic body of thought comparable to that created by the
pragmatists at the end of the century. Professional philosophers
really did not exist as a separate group, and most of the work
a philosophy was carried on by ministers, schoolmasters,
essayists, and poets. Out of this work there emerged two kinds
of philosophy. Each was decidedly religious; each was strongly
influenced by European thought, but still exhibited distinctively
American characteristics. One was academic, orthodox, and
essentially conservative; the other was literary, transcendental,
and potentially radical.

The Academic Mind

At the turn of the nineteenth century the curriculum in
most American colleges was dominated by studies in natural
and moral philosophy. Natural philosophy included the physical
sciences and was very much concerned with efforts to show
how the facts of nature supported a religious view of the
universe. Moral philosophy included the subjects we now think
of as the social sciences. After about 1820 courses in natural
philosophy began to give way to separate courses in natural
science. The moral philosophy course remained. It was supposed
to be the crowning intellectual experience of the student's under-
graduate career and was usually taught by the president of the
college, who was almost always a clergyman.

In the spring of 1829 James Marsh wrote to advise
Coleridge that Locke's works, "formerly much read and used
as textbooks in our colleges," were being replaced by "the
Scotch writers; and Stewart, Campbell and Brown are now
almost universally read as the standard authors on the subjects
of which they treat." It is not difficult to understand why the
teachers of moral philosophy in American colleges developed

a critical attitude toward Locke's philosophy at this time. Orthodox Protestantism controlled most of the important colleges in America during the 1820's, and the religious leaders, whether they were Congregational, Methodist, Baptist, or Presbyterian, still shaken by the effects of their recent struggle with the "infidel philosophy" of Tom Paine and his followers, could not be forever satisfied with a philosopher whose premises were all too often associated with the conclusions of a celebrated atheist like Hume, or with the dangerously idealistic speculations of Berkeley. The Scottish writers were welcomed in America because they offered a sensible, safe philosophy, on the principles of which orthodox doctrines could be securely grounded. Locke had described the mind as a "tabula rasa," and denied the existence of innate ideas. The Scottish writers, however, boldly proclaimed the importance of intuition, through which man was said to gain knowledge of his own mind, the outside world, and the moral law.

Probably the most influential of the "moral philosophers" was Francis Wayland, president of Brown University, whose *Elements of Moral Science* (1835) sold 137,000 copies in thirty years. Wayland's work, like that of many of his contemporaries, shows a blending of Lockian psychology with Scottish philosophy. He sought the basis for his ethical system in the experience of rational creatures rather than in Scripture. Following the example of thinkers like Dugald Stewart, Wayland placed great emphasis on the "moral faculty" of conscience as an autonomous power: "The Conscience can be strengthened not by using the memory, or the taste, or the understanding, but by using the conscience, and by using it precisely according to the laws, and under the conditions, designed by our Creator."

Wayland liked to refer to the moral sense as "our innate inborn gumption," and the homely quality of that definition is revealing. He was not talking about intuition in the transcendental sense. His "gumption," as we shall see, was infinitely more docile and well mannered than Emerson's "over-soul." Wayland and his colleagues have been happily described by Stow Persons as "Protestant Scholastics." They were, above all, Protestant schoolmasters **trying** to synthesize the faith of the seventeenth century with the ideas of the Enlightenment, and their assumption was that a liberal education should naturally confirm the truths of revelation. As Professor Persons points out in his book *American Minds,* the academic philosophers played an important conservative role in the rapidly changing society of mid-nineteenth century America by providing "moral discipline and an ordered conceptual pattern of experience for the educated class of a society that was in the process of dissolving many of the traditional supports of social order and intellectual authority."

Although they exercised a conservative function, the academic philosophers were still representative. Tocqueville observed that "each American appeals to the individual exercise of his own understanding alone. America is therefore one of the countries in the world where philosophy is least studied, and where the precepts of Descartes are best applied." Consciously or not, the professors were trying to build a philosophy out of a behavior pattern common to most Americans. The spirit of the age, however, demanded something more than common sense. Ralph Waldo Emerson, who liked to think of himself as "a transparent eyeball," provided it.

The Transcendental Mind: Emerson

The first thing to make clear about American Transcendentalism as Perry Miller pointed out in the introduction to his anthology on the movement is that it is "most accurately to be defined as a religious demonstration." The participants in this demonstration were young men and women living mostly in the vicinity of Boston who between 1830 and 1840 revolted against Unitarianism. Their spiritual leader was Emerson, and their spiritual roots went deep into the experience of Puritan New England.

Transcendentalism was closely related to Unitarianism. We have already noticed how attractive Channing was to younger men like Emerson and Theodore Parker. They responded to his attempts to dispose of the encumbrances of Calvinist theology, his emphasis on the quality of religious experience and the God-like quality in man. But the spiritualism of Channing was only one aspect of Unitarianism in America. The other aspect, almost exclusively rationalistic, and, by implication, at least, authoritarian, was well illustrated by Professor Andrews Norton at Harvard. The following quotation suggests the quality of Norton's mind:

> He was unwilling to take anything for granted—to believe anything that he could not prove, or for which he had not the testimony of competent witnesses. In the Gospels he rejected every passage, every text, every word, in which he could discover any possible token of interpolation or of error in transcription; and the books thus expurgated he received, because he had convinced himself by research and reasoning that they were the veritable writings of the men whose names they bear, and the authentic record of the life of him whose life they portray. (Andrew Peabody, *Harvard Reminiscences* [Boston, 1888], p. 74.)

It was this second aspect of Unitarianism, the "corpse cold Unitarianism of Brattle Street," Emerson called it, which the transcendentalists rejected for a new faith based on intuition. The "newness" of the new faith, however, must be qualified. In an important essay on Emerson and Jonathan Edwards, Perry Miller has shown how Emerson's quarrel with Unitarianism repeated a pattern set in the religious experience of seventeenth century New England by the two-sided nature of Puritanism. One side of Puritanism, Miller noted, was concerned with "an ideal of social conformity, of law and order, of regulation and control." Another side was essentially mystical and emphasized the individual encounter between man and God at the moment of regeneration. When Anne Hutchinson defied the leaders of the Massachusetts Bay Colony by insisting that she would follow the voice from within rather than the authority from without, she was expressing the mystical or "pietistic" element in Puritanism. A century later Jonathan Edwards repeated the pattern by producing some of his greatest theological treatises to show the primacy of truly religious "affections" and defend the Great Awakening against the attacks of rationalist critics like Charles Chauncy. Emerson's new faith was in the tradition of Anne Hutchinson and Jonathan Edwards. It was a new expression of the old pietism that was not included in Unitarianism. In one sense, then, Transcendentalism in America was an old heresy in new clothes.

Although Transcendentalism was essentially a native growth, European influences upon it were important. European thought helped to shape American Transcendentalism in two different ways. There was, first of all, the Platonic influence. Emerson's idealism, his belief in nature as the expression of spirit, owed much to Plato. His mystical conception of the over-soul was probably influenced by Plotinus. The second important European influence was European Romanticism. From England, the poetry of Wordsworth and Coleridge was especially attractive, emphasizing as it did the importance of feeling and the immanence of God in nature. German philosophy was also important, particularly the work of Kant which attempted to refute the empirical philosophy of Locke and Hume by demonstrating the creative power of the human mind.

Emerson lived from 1803 to 1882, but most of his important work was done between 1832, when he resigned his Unitarian pastorate, and the Civil War. His medium of expression was not the philosophical treatise but the essay and poem, and his most famous essays "Nature," "The American Scholar," "The Divinity School Address," "Self-Reliance," and "The Transcendentalist" appeared between 1836 and 1841.

Emerson came as close to a definition of Transcendentalism as it was possible for him to do in a lecture delivered on the subject in 1842. "What is popularly called transcendentalism among us is Idealism. As thinkers mankind have ever divided into two sects, Materialists and Idealists, the first class founding on experience, the second on consciousness, the first class beginning to think from the data of the senses, the second class perceive that the senses are not final and say, the senses give representations of things, but what are the things themselves they cannot tell. . . . The materialist insists on facts, on history, on the force of circumstances and the animal wants of man; the idealist on the power of thought and of will, on inspiration, on miracle, on individual culture."

Emerson believed that materialists lived according to the

dictates of the Understanding, while idealists (transcendentalists) tried to live according to the dictates of Reason. By the Understanding he meant to refer to the mind of the Enlightenment, the mind of Benjamin Franklin, for example, and of most of Emerson's contemporaries, completely absorbed in the affairs of the world. By Reason (which he also called the *over-soul*) he meant the power of intuition that brings men immediately in touch with God.

Emerson's Reason and Wayland's conscience must be distinguished from each other. Wayland expected that conscience would confirm the Sunday sermon and conventional Protestant morality. Emerson warned that "no doctrine of the Reason" could "bear to be taught by the Understanding," and in a famous address asked the divinity students at Harvard to forget the musty learning of their professors, in order to become new-born bards of the Holy Ghost "and acquaint men at first hand with Deity." When Andrews Norton, the Unitarian "pope," made a violent attack on Emerson in the press, Emerson replied in lofty tones that he had no intention of being drawn into an "argument." That was his way of saying that he would not discuss divine subjects on the level of the Understanding.

Because he believed that nature and God were one, Emerson denied the existence of evil. He did, however, retain the highly developed moral sense of Calvinism, although he never spoke about sin in a way that would have satisfied an orthodox theologian. To the extent that man lived by Reason, so far was he God. To the extent that he did not, he was a God in ruins. He could repair the ruin himself by living from within according to his deepest, most profound intuitions. The important thing was to trust himself. On being warned that these impulses might come from below and not from above Emerson replied, "they do not seem to me to be such, but if I am the Devil's child, I will live then from the Devil. No law can be sacred to me but that of my nature." He could say this only because for him the kingdom of darkness did not exist. Intuition became for Emerson, then, what "divine and supernatural grace" had been for Edwards. The difference is that Edwards believed in a God who only visited his grace on a select few while Emerson believed that all men could embrace ultimate truth by simply recognizing the divine presence already within.

To the orthodox churchmen and academic philosophers of his own time Emerson was a subversive thinker preaching the latest form of infidelity. To a whole generation of restive young intellectuals he was a prophet. In his later years after the Civil War, even though his powers had radically declined, Emerson was generally recognized as the greatest representative of American thought and letters. By the mid-twentieth century, however, his reputation had gone into eclipse largely because Americans who had been forced to experience the savagery of world war and cope with the possibility of nuclear annihilation found it difficult to accept as profound any thinker who refused to take evil seriously.

Two recent studies emphasizing the complexity and depth of his thought go a long way in restoring Emerson to his former eminence. In *Emerson's Angle of Vision* Sherman Paul points out that Emerson sought to solve for his time one of the most profound problems the human mind can conceive— the "relatedness of man and the universe . . . the relation of spirit and matter, of man to nature." Emerson did not turn his back on the real world. He thought of the human mind as "the lens converging the rays of spirit on the daily affairs of man." To Emerson, therefore, every man became a potential philosopher whose integrity as a thinker and a man of action depended on his ability to transmit "influences from the vast and universal to the point on which his genius can act."

Stephen Whicher's *Freedom and Fate* is a sensitive analysis of Emerson's intellectual development which emphasizes the role of conflict and crisis in Emerson's thought. Whicher shows how as a young Unitarian minister Emerson was profoundly troubled by the attacks of Enlightenment philosophers like Hume on historical Christianity. He surrendered his belief in revealed Christianity for a "faith in the soul." This ushered in a period of great exuberance and optimism when he seemed to believe that everything was possible for the man who lived truly from within. "Give me health and a day," he wrote in a characteristic utterance, "and I will make the pomp of Emperors ridiculous." By the latter part of the 1830's, however, Emerson was forced to recognize that no amount of transcendental enthusiasm would make the world over in his lifetime. Whicher characterizes the last forty years of Emerson's life as a period of acquiescence and optimism during which his "belief in the possibilities of man" was tempered by his "perception of man's limitations."

Yet in the end it was the affirmative voice of Emerson that was the source of his power. A society that glorified the free individual could hardly ask for more. "I am *Defeated* all the time; yet to Victory I am born." Whicher quotes the statement as an example of Emerson's extreme optimism. To Americans confronting the expanding opportunities which America offered in the 1830's and 40's it was not extravagant. The psychology of boom and bust left no place for the finality of defeat. It is not surprising that Emerson, for all his abstruseness, and the biting sarcasm which he employed to attack "the smooth mediocrity and squalid contentment of the times" should have been a popular figure on the lecture platform, and that thousands of untutored Americans at mid-century should have flocked to hear him. The rhetoric and mysticism may have been beyond many of them, but the essential doctrine—that man was free and limitless in his powers—had a familiar and happy sound. The one word that does not apply to the new democracy is modesty. Americans were ready to believe in their own divinity.

SCIENCE

In the last paragraph of his book on science in the revolutionary period, Brooke Hindle writes that "the heritage left by the revolutionary generation contained no more important element than this faith that science would flourish in America and that it would be instrumental in advancing the health of the nation." By the time of Jackson, it became clear that America's faith in science was being expressed in a special way. Tocqueville observed that Americans paid great attention to the purely practical part of science "but scarcely anyone [devoted] himself to the essentially theoretical and abstract portion of human knowledge." Ironically enough, the decline in pure science may have been started by the revolution itself. Donald Fleming has pointed out in a perceptive essay that while revolutionaries in France and Germany succeeded in revolutionizing their systems of education, thus contributing to great new developments in science, America "entered the nineteenth century with an unrevolutionized system of education" and an egalitarian philosophy which actually inhibited the development of pure science by undermining the institution of patronage on the part of the rich and well born.

The new nation's concern with practical science can be documented in the astonishing record of American inventiveness in the first half of the century. The infant republic had relied on the imported brains and technical experience of men like Samuel Slater to build its machinery. By mid-century the balance had shifted and the home-grown product was being sent abroad. At the Crystal Palace Exhibition in London in 1851 the McCormick reaper was a source of jest—until the jurors saw it cut down a swathe of wheat 74 yards long in 70 seconds. After it had "mowed down the British prejudice," the reaper drew more visitors in the hall than the famed Koh-i-noor diamond. An English observer, upon leaving the exhibit of Goodyear's products, remarked that the rubber boots were "really seven-league boots" and "fitting symbols of Jonathan who, when he walks a step, necessarily takes the strides of a giant."

By 1851 thousands of American parlors were decorated with a steel engraving entitled "Men of Progress" which included portraits of scientists and inventors like William Morton (ether), Samuel Colt (revolver), Cyrus McCormick, Charles Goodyear, Joseph Henry (electromagnetism), Samuel Morse, Elias Howe, and Richard Hoe (revolving printing press). When President Pierce, in his inaugural address two years later, asked the Congress to give proper recognition "to those men of genius who by their inventions and discoveries in science and arts have contributed largely to the improvements of our age," he was expressing the gratitude of the nation.

It is one thing to document the explosion in American

technology at this time, but something else to explain it. The reasons why Americans applauded the fact are closely related to the spirit of the age. National pride was very much involved. "If we have no Alexander, or Caesar or Bonaparte or Wellington, to shine on the stormy pages of our history," announced one patriot in 1866, "we have such names as Franklin, Whitney, Morse, and a host of others, to shed a more beneficent lustre on the story of our rise. The means by which a few poor colonists have come to excel all nations in the arts of peace, and to astonish the people of Europe with their achievements, through the development of their inventive genius, are true subjects for a history of the United States."

Natural science was particularly popular in America, and Donald Fleming has suggested that the appeal of collecting and classifying specimens of plant and animal life was probably enhanced by the fact that ordinary people could participate in this activity without special training. In addition the activity itself appeared to be "the intellectual aspect of pioneering" by identifying "the canvassing of natural resources" with "mastery of the environment in a new country."

Practical science was also the science of the common man, giving him dominion over nature not, as Channing pointed out, "to exalt a few, but to multiply the comforts and ornaments of life for the multitude of man." The common man's interest in science lay directly behind one of the characteristic institutions of the time, the Lyceum Movement. In 1834 there were 3,000 lyceums in the United States. The popular interest in science was so great that when Benjamin Silliman lectured in Boston on chemistry, crowds jammed the streets outside the lecture hall tightly enough to smash the windows in an adjoining store.

Tocqueville saw a connection in America among social mobility, money, and utility. As the advantages of inherited wealth decreased, the value of money-making increased, with the result that every new method that spared labor and took a shorter route to wealth seemed to be "the grandest effort of human intellect." The successful American scientist made money himself by making it possible for his countrymen to make money more easily. The inhibiting effect of this kind of ethos on the advancement of pure science is clearly observed in the state of American medicine during the period. Richard Shryock in his history of American medical research concludes that "practically no men in this period had what could be called research careers, and no cities were truly research centers. American medical science on the eve of the Civil War was still colonial in nature." Oliver Wendell Holmes's remark that it would be good for mankind but hard on the fishes if most American medicine was thrown into the sea is, perhaps, a little harsh. The fact remains, however, that Morton's work on ether and Beaumont's researches on digestion were striking exceptions to the rule. A speaker at the University of Pennsylvania's Medical School in 1840 claimed that the emphasis on private practice in America was responsible for the absence of the clinical and pathological studies which distinguished French medicine at the time. "Money was in the air," he said, "the only way for a physician to support himself was through practice. Even if the doctor enjoyed independent means, he must seek a fashionable practice for the sake of professional reputation."

The rush of American inventions during this period was stimulated by the attempts of individual citizens to help themselves. Patent drawings in the 1830's, for example, suggest that the American mind and imagination were less engaged in the attempt to improve steam engines or textile manufacture than in the perfection of handicraft tools. In his brilliant study *Mechanization Takes Command* Siegfried Gidieon argues that an essential reason for the explosion in technology is that traditional skills and tools were imported into a new nation, and changed by a people released from traditional restraints.

The settlers brought over their European mode of living, their European experience. But from the origin of the complicated craft and the whole culture in which such institutions had grown, they were suddenly cut off. They had to start from scratch. Imagination was given scope to shape reality unhindered. . . . The axe, the knife, saw, hammer, shovel, the household utensils and appliances, in short the panoply of instruments whose form had remained static for centuries in Europe, are taken up and shaped anew from the first quarter of the nineteenth century on.

From his study of drawings in the United States Patent Office, which he finds to have the quality of folk art, Gidieon describes the multiple refinements of traditional tools and devices (like the scythe, the axe, and the door lock) from 1830 to 1860. We are thus in a position to understand why British immigrants in the 1850's were advised to leave their tools at home. They could find better in a nation whose gaze was, as Agassiz discovered, "wholly turned to the future."

The marriage between religion and science is yet another reason which helps to explain the growth of science and technology during this period. At the start of his career, Asa Gray, who later gained world renown as a botanist, would not travel on the Sabbath. While on a trip to Europe in search of laboratory equipment he refrained from visiting the opera out of religious scruples. To men like Gray, Benjamin Silliman, Joseph Henry, or Louis Agassiz, it would have been absurd to even mention the possibility of a conflict between science and religion. They all assumed that to advance in scientific knowledge was to know more about God's design in the world. In a recent biography of Louis Agassiz, Edward Lurie shows how the famous zoologist's reputation was due in part to his ability to provide "a scientific demonstration of the spiritual quality underlying all material creation." Agassiz liked to describe glacial formations as "God's great plough," and once said that man could come to "a full understanding of Nature" from the very reason that he had "an immortal soul." It is hardly surprising that a generation that looked at Emerson as its first philosopher should have seen Agassiz as its first scientist.

In his book on American science and government Hunter Dupree observes that during Jackson's administration "the old naturalist or natural philosopher who aspired to universal competence was being crushed under such a weight of accumulated knowledge that he perforce became a specialist." The observation is worth noting here because it suggests that for all its pre-Darwinian flavor and emphasis on utility there were important elements of modernity in the science of the period. The founding of the Smithsonian Institution is a case in point. While it is true that the Institution was made possible by an Englishman's bequest and that even then congressmen were reluctant to support it ("What do we care about stuffed snakes and alligators?" grumbled one of them), the importance of its establishment in 1846, with Joseph Henry as secretary, can hardly be overemphasized. Henry was America's ranking physicist. He had previously worked out the principles for the electromagnetic telegraph, but he had been more interested in continuing his research than in its practical applications. Henry's great contribution as an administrator was to insist that the Smithsonian encourage pure as well as applied science. By 1859, in his annual report he felt the Institution could claim success "in rendering familiar to the public mind in the United States the three fundamental distinctions in regard to knowledge, which must have an important bearing on the future advance of science in this country: namely, the *increase* of knowledge, the *diffusion* of knowledge, and the practical *application* of knowledge to useful purposes in the arts."

During the decade of the 1830's eighteen states supported geologic surveys. By the forties and fifties the federal government had taken over a similar role by supporting topographical surveys in the trans-Mississippi west. These expeditions were under the control of the United States Army Engineers, but they usually carried a full complement of civilian scientists including geologists, botanists, and astronomers.

Probably the most important scientific enterprise undertaken by the government before the Civil War was the United States Exploring Expedition (1838-1842). Under the command of Charles Wilkes, an officer in the United States Navy, the expedition surveyed routes in the south seas frequented by American whalers, touched the continent of Antarctica, drew up charts that were useful to our navy even in 1943, and returned with vast collections of scientific material.

By 1860 American expansionism by land and by sea and the establishment of government agencies like the Smithsonian Institution, the Coast Survey, and the Naval Observatory had given the federal government an important position as a patron of science.

We have emphasized the marriage of religion and science

in the American mind at mid-century. This should not obscure the fact of a growing secular-mindedness, a growing tendency, among educated people at least, to look for natural causes behind even the most extraordinary events. When a great comet blazed across American skies in March of 1843, an evangelical sect like the Millerites saw it as a sign of the end of the world. A good many citizens around Boston reacted differently. They raised $25,000 to buy a telescope for Harvard, and four years later the Cambridge Observatory was equal to the best in Europe.

The changing attitude toward disease during this period is also illuminating. The cholera epidemics of 1832 and 1849 were interpreted by most Americans as a visitation of divine wrath, an explanation made plausible by the fact that the disease hit most heavily at the poor, filthy, and criminal elements in the population. By the time of the 1866 epidemic, however, as Charles Rosenberg points out in his study on the subject, "Fast days were beginning to seem the concern of the fanatics," and prayers were giving way before demands to the Public Health Board for chloride of lime, clean privies, and pure water.

It was Darwin, of course, who would threaten to send the tree of faith crashing to the ground, and his impact on American thought is one of the main themes in American intellectual history after the Civil War. This gentle tugging at the roots before the war went largely unnoticed as religion, philosophy, and science continued to reinforce each other.

THREE

Political and Social Thought in the American Democracy

The values shared by American thinkers, excluding Southerners, during the middle of the nineteenth century were much more important than the values over which they differed. The beliefs in individualism, equality, and self-government went essentially unchallenged and constituted what Louis Hartz has called the "liberal consensus" in the American mind. The concept of an American liberal consensus, however, is most useful in helping us to distinguish American thinkers from Europeans; it does not help us a great deal in distinguishing American thinkers from each other. We will do well therefore to consider the consensus not as a monolithic unanimity but as a kind of continuum. At the extreme left of the continuum we can place reformers and radicals like Wendell Phillips and Henry Thoreau. They represent an American brand of radicalism and are set off from their contemporaries by their insistence that social and political conditions in America should instantly conform to the ideals of the Declaration of Independence and the imperatives of conscience and the moral law. At the other end of the continuum are men like Webster and Lincoln who represent an American and democratic brand of conservatism. They give voice to what Daniel Boorstin in his book *The Genius of American Politics* calls "the givenness" of the American experience. They are impressed with the fact that America with all her flaws still incarnates the hope of the world and that any attempts to change her institutions on the basis of abstract notions of truth and justice should be properly suspect. Somewhere in the middle of this continuum, as we shall see, are the Jacksonians, oscillating back and forth between left and right, between reform and conservation. Let us begin with them.

THE MIND OF THE JACKSONIANS

Frederic Bancroft wrote that Andrew Jackson was "the representative for his generation of the American mind." Certainly some understanding of the ideas and values that Jackson expressed or that were identified with him are essential if we are to understand the democratic mind during this period.

Two recent books provide us with a starting point. Marvin Meyers's *The Jacksonian Persuasion* underscores the conservative quality in the Jacksonian mind. Tocqueville described Americans as "venturous conservatives" who wanted change but feared revolution. According to Meyers, Jackson and his followers thought and acted as venturous conservatives. On the one hand they were "boldly liberal in economic affairs out of conviction and appetite combined, and moved their world in the direction of modern capitalism. But they were not inwardly prepared for the grinding uncertainties, the shocking changes, the complexity and indirection of the new economic ways." To support this view Meyers emphasizes what he calls the "restoration theme" in Jackson's messages to Congress. His opponents might call him a king, but Jackson thought of himself as the representative of the whole people and the custodian of traditional American values in a time of tremendous change. The national bank, because its control was not in the hands of the people, symbolized the changes threatening American values. Jackson condemned it as "one of the fruits of a system at war with the genius of all our institutions—a system founded upon a political creed the fundamental principle of which is a distrust of the popular will as a safe regulator of political power."

One of the most interesting and illuminating books written about Jackson in recent years is John William Ward's *Andrew Jackson: Symbol for an Age*. Ward is concerned less with what Jackson himself says or thinks than with what Jackson represents in the minds of masses of Americans. His thesis is that "the symbolic Andrew Jackson is the creation of his time. Through the age's leading figure were projected the age's leading ideas. Of Andrew Jackson the people made a mirror of themselves."

The first of three basic concepts that Ward finds associated with Jackson is related to the idea of nature. Jackson's celebrated victory over the British in the battle of New Orleans was celebrated countless times, in anecdote, oratory, and song, as a victory for men trained in the West, near the soil but close to the forest, over professional British soldiers conscripted from the slums of corrupt European cities. Bancroft called Jackson a "nursling of the wilds" able to rely on "the oracles of his own mind." He was Emerson's self-reliant man, who didn't have to clutter up his mind with artificial learning because he could learn from nature. At this point, politics and transcendentalism merge into one in the democratic mind.

The second concept associated with Jackson in the popular mind was will. Jackson was repeatedly characterized as a "man of iron." His indomitable will and personal courage were emphasized in accounts of the several duels he fought. His orphaned youth was taken as a sign that he willed his own success. The prompt manner in which he dispatched Arbuthnot and Ambrister in Florida, and his resolute opposition to nullification in South Carolina were interpreted as signs of Jackson's iron resolve to stand up for the right no matter what the cost.

If Jackson was the "man of iron," he was also "God's Right-hand Man." Ward shows how Americans saw mirrored in him their own belief in divine providence. Evidence to support this idea is easy to find in Jackson's life: his seemingly miraculous victory at New Orleans and even more miraculous escape when an assassin's pistol misfired twice in succession at point-blank range are only two of countless examples which seemed to indicate that God had picked him out for a special destiny.

One of the advantages of approaching intellectual history through myth and symbol, as Ward does, is that it helps us see the elements of contradiction and paradox which have always been present in American thought. The celebration of human will is hardly consistent with a belief in Providence, yet both ideas were of central importance to Americans in the pre-Civil War period, a time when men could place unbounded confidence in their own efforts to improve a world controlled by God.

We have been talking thus far about three important preoccupations of the American mind during the Jacksonian period. These are: first, that Americans are more virtuous and more powerful than Europeans because they are closer to nature; second, that Americans can accomplish great things in the world on the basis of determination and will; third, that a benevolent God presides over the glorious destiny of the American people. A simple faith in the people is a common theme in all three concepts and it was this faith that Jackson expressed in his first message to Congress when he said "policy requires that as few impediments as possible should exist to the free operation of the public will." Jackson's assault on chartered monopolies, his support of popular suffrage and rotation in office, his concern, in other words, for the democratization of American economics and politics, grew out of this fundamental belief. Jackson, however, was a man more suited to action than philosophy, and like many great men he had intellectual followers more capable than he of articulating the principles on which he operated. William Leggett and George Bancroft were such men.

Leggett, who lived from 1802 to 1839 and worked for several years with William Cullen Bryant on the New York *Evening Post,* was a vigorous proponent of the economic liberalism associated with the Jacksonians. Like Jackson himself, Leggett was offended by the tendency of state governments to rely on chartered monopolies as a way of encouraging internal improvements. "Not a road can be opened, not a bridge can be built, not a canal can be dug," he lamented, "but a charter of exclusive privileges must be granted for the purpose . . . the bargaining and trucking away of chartered privileges is the whole business of our lawmakers." Leggett argued that exclusive charters represented a violation of the principle of equality. He believed that the arguments for universal manhood suffrage could be applied to economic activity. A man should not be shut out of certain enterprises because he possessed too little capital to be chartered by the state. What Leggett wanted was a government that contented itself with protecting the persons and property of its citizens, and left them free to pursue whatever economic activity their talents might dictate.

Their only safeguard against oppression is a system of legislation which leaves to all the free exercise of their talents and industry, within the limits of the GENERAL LAW, and which, on no pretence of public good, bestows on any particular class of industry, or any particular body of men, rights or privileges not equally engaged by the great aggregate of the body politic.

Leggett was opposed to banks because they were chartered. He even had some doubts about the wisdom of a publicly sponsored post office, and although he encouraged the organization of workingmen's associations he felt that the price of labor should be absolutely determined by the market.

From one point of view Leggett's ideas express the liberalism of the Jacksonians. He sought to make the economy more democratic, to open up the opportunities for profit, opportunities far greater than had ever existed before, to little as well as large capitalists. From another point of view Leggett seems traditional. Like the Jeffersonians before him, he believed in the sanctity of private property and the impropriety of the state's attempting to play a positive role in social and economic change.

George Bancroft was born in Worcester in 1800. His father was a liberal Congregational minister and a Federalist. Bancroft graduated from Harvard in 1817, just four years before Emerson, and partly on the basis of his prize-winning essay, "The Use and Necessity of Revelation," was sent to Germany for theological study. In Germany he met Goethe, Schleiermacher, and Hegel; in Paris, D'Alembert and Von Humboldt; and on the Mediterranean coast, Byron, the most romantic figure of the age. Bancroft spent six years in Europe soaking up German philosophy, taking on European manners, and drifting steadily away from the Syriac and Hebrew grammar he had come to study. When he finally returned to Cambridge the professors of the Harvard Divinity School, discovering their mistake, snorted in disgust and turned away. For the next few years Bancroft taught school in Northampton, Massachusetts. By the 1830's he had become active in the Jacksonian movement in Massachusetts, thus launching a political career that later brought him major political and diplomatic appointments. In 1834 Bancroft published the first of his ten-volume *History of the United States,* covering the period between the discovery of America and the close of the Revolutionary War. Bancroft's career as an historian was repeatedly interrupted by political and diplomatic assignments, and it took him more than forty years to complete his history. An indication of its popularity may be found in the fact that the first volume is said to have found its way into one third of all the homes in New England within a year of its publication.

Bancroft's philosophy of history, a blending of transcendental and Jacksonian ideas, is clearly expressed in an oration he delivered in 1835 entitled "The Office of the People." Like Emerson, Bancroft sought to distinguish between the higher and lower faculties of the mind: the higher faculty is reason, "not that faculty which deduces inferences from the experience of the senses, but that higher faculty, which from the infinite treasury of its own consciousness, originates truth and assents to it by the force of intuitive evidence." The existence of reason within every man justified the reliance that Jackson and his supporters placed on the will of the people. "Our free institutions have reversed the false and ignoble distinctions between men," Bancroft said, "and refusing to gratify the pride of caste, have acknowledged the common mind to be the true material for a commonwealth."

We have already noticed that Jackson was associated in the popular mind with the concept of Providence. To Bancroft the history of the American experience was providential in every respect. God intended men to progress toward a condition of more perfect freedom, truth, justice, and morality, and America would lead the way for the rest of the world. American history from Columbus to Andrew Jackson was simply the breaking of greater and greater light into the world.

The spirit of God breathes through the combined intelligence of the people. Truth is not to be ascertained by the impulses of an individual; it emerges from the contradiction of personal opinions; it raises itself in majestic serenity above the strife of parties and the conflict of sects; it acknowledges neither the solitary mind nor the separate faction as its oracle; but owns as its only faithful interpretation the dictates of pure reason, itself, proclaimed by the general voice of mankind.

THE REFORM IMPULSE

In the fall of 1841 a great congress of social reformers convened in Boston's Chardon Street Chapel. A little paper in an adjoining village described the occasion:

Since the day of Pentecost, we don't believe such a conglomeration of strange tongues has ever been known. All sorts of things were said by all sorts of persons on all sorts of subjects. Clergymen were there as well as laymen, Trinitarians and Unitarians, Transcendentalists and Latterists, Universalists and Calvinists, Methodists and Baptists, Atheists and Deists, Mormons and Socialists, white men and black men, men with beards and men without, no-money men and anti-property men, Cape Cod Come-outers and Latter Day Saints, Jews and Quakers, Dialists and Plain Speakers, Unionists and Perfectionists, Non Resistants, Abolitionists, Women Lecturers, Owenites, Grahamites, and all the Ists and Ites, the contented and discontented *ons* and *ans* that make up this queer compound called the world.

The spirit of reform swept across the American landscape in the thirties and forties as never before or since. There were so many reformers around Boston that some boardinghouses catered exclusively to them. The American mind during this period, at least in the North and West, but especially in New England, was preoccupied with schemes for moral and social reform.

Why should so many Americans have become engrossed in reform projects during the thirty years before the Civil War? Alice Felt Tyler gives the traditional answer to this question when she writes in *Freedom's Ferment* that "the militant democracy of the period was a declaration of faith in man and in the perfectibility of his institutions. . . . The desire to perfect human institutions was the basic cause for each sect and community, and this same desire lay at the roots of all the many social reform movements of the period."

The perfectionism of the American democratic faith had a political, religious, and mythical dimension. Politically it owed more to the idealism of Jefferson and the Declaration of Independence than to the hard-headed realism of the men who wrote the Constitution. The faith in equality and natural rights descending through the Jeffersonian tradition was intensified by the optimism of the Jacksonians. Jackson himself was strongly opposed to humanitarian reform movements like abolitionism, but the faith in the common people which he espoused strengthened the reformer's hand. A people capable of exercising total political power was obviously good enough to be made better.

The perfectionist faith was profoundly religious. During the early nineteenth century when the doctrines of natural depravity and predestination were replaced by the belief that men could contribute to their own salvation, it grew stronger and was given particularly powerful impetus by the evangelical preaching of men like Finney during the second Great Awakening. Finney insisted that the transforming grace of Christianity be applied to worldly affairs. John Humphrey Noyes was so powerfully affected by Finney's preaching, and so confident of the possibility of pure holiness in this world, that he founded the Oneida Community, which did away with every kind of private relationship including private property and the marriage contract. Noyes was an extremist even among reformers, but the perfectionist emphasis that Finney and his co-workers left in their trail had a profound effect on reform movements, especially upon the abolitionists in the 1830's. Theodore Dwight Weld, who did as much as any man to spread antislavery societies throughout upper New York State and Ohio, was a Finney disciple, and John Thomas has shown in a recent biography how fundamental the perfectionist faith was to William Lloyd Garrison, best known of all the abolitionists.

Transcendentalism was itself a perfectionist philosophy. Emerson taught that every man in his natural state was a God in ruins, and could by following his own most profound insights become divine. By temperament Emerson was more the philosopher and critic than the reformer, but his ideas were food and drink to other restless spirits who sought to build an earthly paradise in ante-bellum America.

Perfectionism also flourished during this period because it articulated what Americans thought America should be. Ever since Henry Nash Smith published *Virgin Land* in 1950, American scholars have been paying increased attention to the importance of myth and symbol in American history. The assumption underlying these recent studies, borrowed from anthropology, is that every people, no matter how primitive or civilized, expresses its most profound convictions and aspirations through myths. Smith found that a dominant symbol for nineteenth century Americans was the myth of the American West as "the garden of the world." The myth of the garden embraced "a cluster of metaphors expressing fecundity, growth, increase, and blissful labor in the earth, all centering about the heroic figure of the frontier farmer armed with that supreme agrarian weapon, the sacred plow." R. W. B. Lewis in *The American Adam* has contended that the central image in nineteenth century American thought was "that of the authentic American as a figure of heroic innocence and vast potentialities, poised at the start of a new history," and Charles L. Sanford in *The Quest for Paradise* calls the myth of America as a new Eden "the most powerful and comprehensive organizing force in American culture."

If the myth of America as an earthly paradise has been an important unifying force in our culture, and has operated in the popular mind as well as at the level of our most imaginative writers, it is easier to understand the American predilection for reform. Schemes intended to reform American society became congenial because America was supposed to be pure. Professor Sanford believes that the effectiveness of the abolitionist appeal to Americans in the North and West can be understood in these terms. "With the threat of the extension of slavery and a semi-feudal social order into this holy region [The Garden of the West] all reforms were swept up by the great cause of Abolition. Fear of sabotage of the American mission by a conspiratorial devil was summed up in the northern indictment of the slave-holder."

To explain the reform impulse in terms of the democratic faith is to emphasize the continuity of ideas in America. It does not explain, however, why American abolitionists, for example, flourished in the 1830's and 40's but not in the 1820's. David Donald has suggested that the answer may be found in the social dislocation of rural Congregational-Presbyterian families during the earlier period. Faced with the loss of status and community leadership to members of a new industrial class, these men and women may have turned to reform in order to maintain their traditional influence in public life. Professor Donald's hypothesis is interesting but remains unproven and is rejected by Louis Filler in the most recent history of the antislavery movement.

Another attempt to link the reform impulse to the American social process can be found in Stanley Elkins's recent book on slavery. Elkins seeks to relate the intensity of the reform impulse to the lack of conservative institutions in American democracy. According to Elkins, American reform activity during the period was characterized by "the absence of clear institutional arrangements for channeling radical energy." Unlike his European counterpart who traditionally worked through the church, labor union, or university, the American reformer was usually an "intellectual without connections," who transformed social wrong into an "individual burden" and took his cause to the people at large with the same kind of rhetoric, propaganda, and passion that typified political campaigns. The American in reform as in everything else was intensely individualistic, and reform movements, which proliferated without developing institutional strength, served less as vehicles for necessary social change than as instruments to dramatize moral issues, inflame the passions of the people, and divide the nation.

Among other things, Professor Elkins's challenging essay is a conservative tract. Whether or not too much democracy helped plunge Americans into civil war is highly debatable. The connection between democracy and reform seems less open to dispute. The society which tended to remove institutional restraints on Americans in order to maximize individual opportunities in politics and economics also tended to maximize individual opportunities to make the world over.

Whatever the confusion of causes that helped create them, American reformers were more numerous and articulate during the thirty years before the Civil War than at any other time in our history. Some of them were death-dealing fanatics like John Brown. Some of them were harmless eccentrics, who believed that simple remedies like cold water baths and a diet of coarse bread might regenerate the world. Others were critics and crusaders of rare insight and eloquence. Two outstanding representatives of the last group are Henry Thoreau, the preeminent social critic among American Transcendentalists, and Wendell Phillips, the intellectual spokesman for American abolitionists.

Henry Thoreau—The Transcendentalist as Critic and Reformer

The external journey of Thoreau is easily summarized. He was born at Concord, Massachusetts, in 1817. After graduating from Harvard University he worked sporadically as a teacher, tutor, handyman, pencil-maker, and surveyor. He wrote steadily throughout his life but was never able to support himself by writing. His first book *A Week on the Concord and Merrimack Rivers* was published in 1845 and received almost no reader response. His famous essay on civil disobedience was published in an obscure transcendentalist journal in 1849, and the classic *Walden,* which appeared in 1854, was silently received. Thoreau died of tuberculosis in 1862.

Thoreau's inner path, the life recorded in his books, essays, and poems, is much more subtle and complicated than the relatively simple furrow which he cut in the affairs of the world. Although Thoreau thought of himself not primarily as a naturalist or social critic but as a literary artist, it is the body of his political and social thought that must primarily concern us.

Thoreau once wrote that "the whole duty of life is contained in the question how to respire and aspire both at once." The quotation provides an appropriate starting point for us because it suggests the main concern of Thoreau's life—to live life as freely and fully as possible without denying the imperatives of conscience. When Thoreau built his solitary cabin at Walden Pond, he did not want to escape the world but to

live deliberately, to front only the essential facts of life and see if I could not learn what it had to teach and not, when I came to die, discover that I had not lived. . . . I wanted to live deep and suck out all the marrow of life, to live so Spartan-like as to put to rout all that was not life, to cut a broad swathe and shave close, to drive life into a corner, and reduce it to its lowest terms, and if it proved to be mean, why then to get the whole and genuine meanness of it and publish its meanness to the world; or if it were sublime, to know it by experience and be able to give a true account of it in my next excursion.

Thoreau said that he came into the world to live in it and not to make it better. He believed that life itself should be an art. "To affect the quality of the day, that is the highest of arts. Every man is tasked to make his life, even in its details, worthy of the contemplation of his most elevated and critical hour." He left the woods, he said, for as good a reason as he came, because he had "several more lives to live, and could not spare any more time for that one."

Usually described as a disciple of Emerson, Thoreau was too crusty to be any man's disciple. Emerson once said that he would no sooner take Thoreau's arm than he would "take the arm of an elm tree," and that his friend never seemed to feel himself "except in opposition." It is probably true that no American ever affirmed the possibilities of life more eloquently, and no one was ever more disappointed in his countrymen than Henry Thoreau.

He found it difficult to comprehend the value system of his contemporaries. The emphasis on personal achievement and material gain, for example, was a constant irritation. "The ways by which you may get money," he said, "almost without exception lead downward. To have done anything by which you earned money *merely* is to have been truly idle." There was still much of the Puritan in Thoreau's strong sense of moral principle, but he complained that the gospel of hard work which had grown out of the Protestant ethic was putting blinders on Americans. The man who loved to spend his time walking in the woods was dismissed as a loafer. If he would only spend his time as a speculator "shearing off those woods and making earth bald before her time" he would be known as a virtuous and enterprising citizen. "As if a town had no interest in its forests but to cut them down!"

The social corollary to personal achievement is progress, and here, too, Thoreau filed a dissenting vote. "Men think that it is essential that the *Nation* have commerce, and export ice, and talk through a telegraph, and ride thirty miles an hour," he complained, "but whether we should live like baboons or like men is a little uncertain." When a railroad was built connecting Chicago and Boston, he called it an "improved means to an unimproved end." Thoreau was an expert on railroads, for he had watched the trains daily from the banks of Walden Pond. Others saw the railroad as the majestic symbol of progress, a great new servant for man. To Thoreau it looked just the other way. "We do not ride on the railroad," he announced, "it rides upon us." Every tie supporting the rails represented the body of a man. The industrial revolution was just beginning and a generation of Americans was eager to be swept along with it. Still America was overwhelmingly rural; mechanization had not yet taken command. What is so remarkable about Thoreau's criticism is that he saw the threat at the outset. He believed that men who chose to tinker with the machine rather than tinker with their own lives and thus "improve the quality of the day," were walking in their sleep. They would not live deliberately and front only the essential facts of life. And when they came to die (like the Irishmen laborers who were memorialized in the railroad ties) many would find they had not lived.

It is easy to oversimplify Thoreau's economic and social ideas. His emphasis on simplicity was not meant to imply a return to primitivism. "There are two kinds of simplicity," he wrote, "one that is akin to foolishness, the other to wisdom. The philosopher's style of living is only outwardly simple, but inwardly complex. The savage's style of living is both outwardly and inwardly simple." Leo Stoller in *After Walden: Thoreau's Changing Views on Economic Man* argues persuasively that as Thoreau grew older he recognized the necessity for accepting the industrial revolution and groped "for methods by which the new system of production could be combined with the noble aim of self culture." He never found the solution he sought, but his search provides some of the most fruitful reading in the whole history of American thought.

Thoreau's political ideas were rooted both in the American revolutionary tradition and in transcendental philosophy. His whole life can be taken as a personal declaration of independence. It was no accident that he began his sojourn at Walden on the Fourth of July. His essay "Civil Disobedience" begins with a quotation from Jefferson, and Thoreau makes a specific analogy between the revolution in 1776, when Americans were unjustly taxed, and the current situation when their conscience was outraged by the Mexican War. The state undertook to tax Thoreau to help support the Congregational Church in Concord. He refused, and at the request of the local selectmen signed a statement in which he applied the principle of government by consent to all organizations. "Know all men by these present, that I, Henry Thoreau, do not wish to be regarded as a member of any incorporated society which I have not joined." If he had known how to name them he would have signed off in detail from all the organizations he had never signed on to, but he did not know where to find a complete list.

"The only obligation which I have a right to assume," Thoreau said, "is to do at any time what I think right." Like Emerson he believed that a man should follow his conscience no matter what the cost and, unlike such eighteenth century moralists as Paley and Franklin, he knew that the moral course would not always be expedient. "If I have unjustly wrested a plank from a drowning man, I must restore it to him though I drown myself. This, according to Paley, would be inconvenient. But he that would save his life, in such a case, shall lose it." It was his devotion to duty that made Thoreau refuse to pay taxes to a state which tolerated slavery, which sent him to the Concord jail for one night, and which in 1859 led him to give a public speech in defense of John Brown.

A good deal has been made of Thoreau's alleged anarchism, but we should remember that when he said "that government is best which governs not at all," he added the qualifying phrase, "when men are prepared for it, that will be the kind of government which they will have." For the most part Thoreau was content with American political institutions. On the one hand, he said, "This state and this American government are, in many respects, very admirable and rare things, to be thankful for." But when loyalty to state collided with loyalty to the higher law, Thoreau knew what his duty was. Jefferson had said "The sober second choice of the people is always right." George Bancroft, in his own way as much a transcendentalist as Thoreau, believed that the higher law was expressed collectively, that "the voice of the people is the voice of God." Thoreau's conception of morality remained entirely individualistic. "I think we should be men first," he said, "and subjects afterwards." When matters of conscience were involved he had no patience with political process. Voting was quantitative, an adding of numbers, a playing with right and wrong. What did it matter what the polls reported on a moral issue, when any man more right than his neighbor constituted a majority of one already?

"Cast your whole vote, not a strip of paper merely, but your whole influence." Thoreau had tried to follow his own advice when he refused to pay a tax to support an unjust war. He was locked up for the night in the Concord jail and let out the next day. Instead of making a speech he set off to lead a huckleberry party. Most of his neighbors thought he was a crank, and even Emerson was mystified.

What Thoreau had done seems innocuous enough. An action which could barely stir a ripple in Concord would hardly shake the foundations in Washington. And yet the principle he enunciated was as potentially powerful and subversive of public order as anything ever written by an American.

A minority is powerless while it conforms to the majority; it is not even a minority then; but it is irresistible when it clogs by its whole weight. If the alternative is to keep all just men in prison, or give up war and slavery, the State will not hesitate which to choose. If a thousand men were not to pay their tax bills this year, that would not be a violent and bloody measure, as it would be to pay them, and enable the state to commit violence and shed innocent blood. This is, in fact, the definition of a peaceable revolution, if any such is possible. If the tax gatherer, or any other public officer, asks me, as one has done, "But what shall I do?" my answer is, "If you really wish to do anything, resign your office." When the subject has refused allegiance, and the officer has resigned his office, then the revolution is accomplished.

Thoreau advocated the doctrine of civil disobedience because it was consistent with his belief that reform could not be imposed from the outside but had to start with the individual and that only as individuals performed their duty would society be transformed. There is some evidence to suggest, however, that in the later years of his life Thoreau's rigid individualism began to soften as he moved toward a view of society which recognized, according to Leo Stoller, "that the success of the single man in his private life was dependent on the success of the community in their social life."

His impact on later generations, however, derives mainly from the moral absolutism of his thought. Few people took Thoreau seriously when he lived. In the twentieth century Gandhi demonstrated the shattering effectiveness of civil disobedience on a massive scale. Today the idea has returned to America, and Thoreau, a man who found the reformers of his own generation distasteful and the thought of attracting disciples of his own abhorrent, has become an ideological sponsor for the civil rights movement in America.

Wendell Phillips—The Rationale for Agitation*

Wendell Phillips was born in Boston in 1811. His family which descended from the first generation of Boston Puritans was as aristocratic as a native-born American's could be. Like other well-born Bostonians he attended Boston Latin School and Harvard College, where he stayed on to earn a law degree. Following a half-hearted attempt to practice law, he became interested in the antislavery movement. In 1837, after the killing of Elijah Lovejoy, an antislavery editor in Illinois, Phillips made a speech in Faneuil Hall which immediately gave him a position of leadership among New England abolitionists. Thereafter he worked closely with William Lloyd Garrison and his supporters. By mid-century he was nationally famous as one of the most effective orators in the country and the leading intellectual in the antislavery movement. He thought of himself, however, more as a reformer or agitator than as an abolitionist, and was as active in reform causes after the war (he lived until 1884) as before it.

* Parts of this section have been adapted from Irving H. Bartlett, "The Persistence of Wendell Phillips," in Martin Duberman, ed., *The Anti-Slavery Vanguard: New Essays on the Abolitionists* (Princeton, N.J.: Princeton University Press, 1965).

Phillips was typical of antislavery reformers in that his career was nourished by religious conviction and by his sense of the American revolutionary tradition. He had been brought up as a devout Calvinist, and he found in abolitionism the calling he could not find in the law. "None know what it is to live," he wrote in 1841, "till they redeem life from its seeming monotony by laying it a sacrifice on the altar of some great cause." Phillips never repudiated his Calvinist belief, but when the New England churches refused to join the abolitionists, he withdrew from membership and joined the other "come outers" then swelling the ranks of the reform movement. Like other abolitionists who believed that abolitionism was a sacred religious cause, Phillips believed in the higher law and judged every public question from an absolute moral standard. Convinced that anything right in principle had to be right in practice, he accepted Garrison's demand for immediate emancipation without question and supported the radical view that unless the North seceded from the Union abolitionists should not vote or hold office. The reasoning behind this was that the government collaborated with slaveholders by protecting the Southern states from slave insurrections and by returning fugitive slaves. Therefore anyone supporting the federal government supported evil and was guilty himself. Such reasoning was typical of the intense, personal moralism which Stanley Elkins and others have said typified American reform in the ante-bellum period.

Phillips never doubted that the revolutionary fathers like his Puritan forebears were on his side. His first antislavery speech supported John Quincy Adams's attempt to get the Congress to hear petitions attacking slavery. Phillips argued that the right of petition was a traditional right for free men and that in attacking it the South threatened the freedom of all men. "This is the reason we render to those who ask us why we are contending against southern slavery," he said, "*that it may not result in northern slavery.* . . . it is our own rights which are at issue."

Phillips's moralism and the assurance that he was supported by the American revolutionary tradition supplied the ballast for his career. His solutions to difficult problems were "right," simple, and "American." When he continued to badger the government long after Garrison and other abolitionists had retired from the field after the war, it was because he sought "*justice*—absolute, immediate, unmixed justice to the negro." He did not, however, live by shibboleths alone, and his tactics as a reformer were based on a surprisingly sophisticated conception of American politics and society.

Phillips recognized that slavery was a threat to the freedom of all Americans. This conviction developed gradually out of his early experiences. He had the grisly reminiscences of friends from the South like Sarah and Angelina Grimké to remind him of the evils of Southern slavery, the whippings and mutilations, the ruthless separation of husband and wife, of parent and child. Closer to his personal experience was what slavery had done to supposedly free American citizens. It had jailed Prudence Crandall for opening a school for Negro girls in Centerbury, Connecticut. It had publicly whipped Amos Dresser for daring to distribute antislavery literature in Nashville, Tennessee. It had tried to gag John Quincy Adams in Congress, had mobbed Garrison within the shadow of Faneuil Hall, and had finally killed Lovejoy in Alton, Illinois. The pattern seemed always to be the same; principle was overcome by power. For the first time Phillips sensed the demonic possibilities of a slave power supported by public opinion in America.

A lawyer, bred in all the technical reliance on the safeguards of Saxon liberty, I was puzzled, rather than astounded, by the fact that, outside of the law and wholly unrecognized in the theory of our institutions, was a mob power—and abnormal element which nobody had counted in, in the analysis of the system, and for whose irregular actions no check, no balance, had been provided. The gun which was aimed at the breast of Lovejoy on the banks of the Mississippi brought me to my feet conscious that I stood in the presence of a power whose motto was victory or death.

Having recognized the importance of public opinion in America, Phillips began to examine American institutions more closely. He distinguished a fundamental tension between the American ideal, a society based on the rights of man, and an

American political system, based on numbers. "The majority rules, and law rests on numbers, not on intellect or virtue," thus "while theoretically holding that no vote of the majority can authorize injustice, we practically consider public opinion the real test of what is true and what is false; and hence, as a result, the fact which Tocqueville has noticed, that practically our institutions protect, not the interest of the whole community, but the interests of the majority."

Phillips was acute enough to see that while the tyranny of the majority might occasionally express itself violently, as in the lynching of Lovejoy, a more common and insidious threat to liberty came through the intimidation of citizens holding unpopular ideas. "Entire equality and freedom in political forms" naturally tended to "make the individual subside into the mass, and lose his identity in the general whole." In an aristocratic society like England a man could afford to "despise the judgment" of most people so long as he kept the good opinion of those in his own class. In America there was no refuge. Every citizen "in his ambition, his social life, or his business" depended on the approbation and the votes of those around him. Consequently, Phillips said, "instead of being a mass of individuals, each one fearlessly blurting out his own convictions,—as a nation, compared with other nations, we are a mass of cowards. More than any other people, we are afraid of each other."

Although Phillips knew that in some nations public opinion was shaped by political leaders, he could find nothing to show that this was true in the American experience. Theoretically every American male citizen was supposed to be eligible for office, but in practice, "with a race like ours, fired with the love of material wealth," the best brains were drawn into commerce. As a result politics recruited "men without grasp enough for large business . . . men popular because they have no positive opinions." Even if an occasional man of the first rank (a Charles Sumner, for example) did emerge in politics, he would be lost to the reformer because the whole art of politics in America was based on the ability to compromise. "The politician must conceal half his principles to carry forward the other half," Phillips said, "must regard, not rigid principle and strict right, but only such a degree of right as will allow him at the same time to secure *numbers.*"

These considerations led Phillips to conclude that the reformer in America had to confront the people directly. "Our aim," he said in his lecture "The Philosophy of Abolitionism," "is to alter public opinion." Slavery endured and abolitionists were mobbed because a majority of Americans refused to face the moral issues involved. Phillips was too much of a realist to believe that he could suddenly convert the nation, but he did feel that he could force the issue and change the public attitude toward slavery.

Phillips knew that most people in the North disliked slavery, but he also knew that it was to their self-interest to leave it alone. To stir up controversy was dangerous: no one wanted to be known as a trouble-maker; mill owners were concerned for their capital; mill hands were concerned for their jobs; the respectable middle class was concerned for its reputation. The easy thing for everyone was to turn away from the problem. The abolitionist's job was to scatter thorns on the easy road by dramatizing the moral issue and insisting that every man who did not throw his whole influence into the scales against slavery was as guilty as the slaveholder. "We will gibbet the name of every apostate so black and high," Phillips warned, "that his children's children shall blush to hear it. Yet we bear no malice —cherish no resentment. We thank God that the love of fame is shared by the ignoble."

What this could mean in practice is perhaps best seen in Phillips's criticism of Henry Gardner, a Boston politician who was the leader of Know-Nothingism in Massachusetts and governor of the commonwealth from 1855 to 1858. Gardner usually made a few antislavery sounds during election campaigns, but his great appeal was to nativism, and it was he who had blocked Phillips's attempt to get Judge Henry Loring recalled after the fugitive slave Anthony Burns was returned to slavery. Phillips believed that Gardner dabbled in antislavery politics for personal gain and frustrated the abolitionists' effort to educate the public. He called the governor "a consummate hypocrite, a man who if he did not have some dozen and distinct reasons for telling the truth would naturally tell a lie." On another occasion he said, "Our course is a perfect copy of Sisyphus. We always toil up, up, up the hill until we touch the soiled sandals of some Governor Gardner, and then the rock rolls down again. Always some miserable reptile that has struggled into power in the corruption of parties—reptiles who creep where *man* disdains to climb; some slight thing of no consequence till its foul mess blocks our path; and dashes our hopes at the last minute."

The denunciation could hardly have been more savage. Phillips insisted, however, that there was nothing personal in it.

Do not say I am personal in speaking thus of Governor Gardner. . . . Do not blame me when I speak thus of Henry J. Gardner. What is the duty of the minority . . . what is the duty of a minority in this country? A minority has no right to rebel . . . the majority have said the thing shall be so. It is not to resist, it is to convert. And how shall we convert? If the community is in love with some monster, we must paint him truly. The duty of a minority being to convert, every tool which the human mind knows, it is their right and duty to use; a searching criticism, pitiless sarcasm, bitter invective, rigid analysis of motives, constant recurrence to the admitted facts of a man's career—these are our rights, if our function is to save the people from delusion.

Phillips was not a fanatic. He used the most violent language as dispassionately as a surgeon uses the sharpest steel. He could not actually cut away the diseased tissue with his rhetoric, but he could expose it. Thus when he called Lincoln a "slave hound" he was reminding his listeners and readers that as a congressman Lincoln had supported a bill that would have enforced the return of fugitive slaves escaping into the District of Columbia. This was the man who expected to get the antislavery vote. Phillips's intention in attacking Lincoln so savagely was simply to dramatize the rottenness of the American conscience by showing that only a "slave hound" could be elected President. His reply to those who accused him of extravagance and distortion was that "there are far more dead hearts to be quickened, than confused intellects to be cleared up—more dumb dogs to be made to speak than doubting consciences to be enlightened. We have use, then, sometimes, for something beside argument."

The easiest way to treat nettlesome reformers like the abolitionists is to dismiss them as cranks. Nothing irritated Phillips more than the attempts of his opponents to thrust him outside the mainstream of American life. The antislavery agitation, he insisted, was "an essential part of the machinery of the state . . . not a disease nor a medicine . . . the normal state of the nation."

The preceding statement takes us to the heart of Phillips's philosophy of reform. He recognized that American ideals could ultimately be translated into practice only through politics. He also knew that the American politician's ability to gain and hold power was largely determined by his ability to effect compromises that appealed to numbers rather than to principle. He added to these corruptive tendencies the fact that people in a democracy always tend to have as high an opinion of themselves as possible—always tremble on the edge of national idolatry. The result, Phillips argued, was that "every government is always growing corrupt. Every Secretary of State is by the very necessity of his position an apostate." A democratic society that trusted to constitutions and political machinery to secure its liberties never would have any. "The people must be waked to a new effort," he said, "just as the church has to be regenerated in each age." In the middle of the nineteenth century the abolitionist was the agency of national regeneration, but even after he had vanished his function in the American system would still remain.

Eternal vigilance is the price of liberty: power is ever stealing from the many to the few. The manna of popular liberty must be gathered each day, or it is rotten. . . . The hand entrusted with power becomes, either from human depravity or *esprit de corps,* the necessary enemy of the people. Only by continual oversight can the democrat in office be prevented from hardening into a despot: only by unintermitted agitation can a people be kept sufficiently awake to principle not to let liberty be smothered in material prosperity. All clouds, it is said, have sunshine behind them, and all evils have some good result; so slavery, by the necessity of its abolition, has saved the freedom of the white race from being melted in luxury or buried beneath the gold of its own success. Never look, therefore, for an age when the people can be quiet and safe. At such times despotism, like a shrouding mist, steals over the mirror of Freedom.

In other words Wendell Phillips, as eloquent and persistent a fighter for good causes as America has ever had, believed that the radical abolitionist was justified as much by his radicalism as by his abolitionism, and that he could never retire from the field if the American mission were to be fulfilled.

CONSERVATISM AND DEMOCRACY

When Nathan Appleton described the beginnings of the cotton mills at Lowell, he remembered how afraid Americans had been that a factory system of labor would threaten traditional values. "The operatives in the manufacturing cities of Europe were notoriously of the lowest character for intelligence and morals. The question therefore arose and was deeply considered, whether this degradation was the result of the peculiar occupation, or of other and distinct causes." Coming from solid Puritan stock, Appleton and his associates refused to admit that hard work could corrupt anyone. They set about, therefore, to find "a fund of labor, well educated and virtuous." Here was the beginning of the famous experiment at Lowell, when the looms were tended by rosy-cheeked farm girls, who left the factories at night to stay at boardinghouses established by the company "under the charge of respectable women, with every provision for religious worship."

This aspect of the early factory movement in America is instructive, for it shows that the men most actively engaged in changing American society during the first half of the nineteenth century were frequently conservative at heart. We have already noticed the extent to which this generalization can be applied to Jackson. The fact that Appleton was a Whig and Jackson a Democrat points up the difficulty of trying to identify conservatism with party lines and suggests the truth of Tocqueville's assertion that the typical American was a "venturous conservative."

Of the many books on conservatism published in America since the Second World War probably the most intelligent and most readable is Clinton Rossiter's *Conservatism in America.* Rossiter contends that the men who opposed extension of the suffrage in the constitutional conventions of 1820, men like Justice Story in Massachusetts and Chancellor Kent in New York, represented "the last and most outspoken stand of genuine, anti-democratic conservatism as a major force in the life of the whole nation." The American political tradition generally, characterized by optimism, idealism, and a belief in progress, has been a liberal tradition. Within the dominantly liberal tradition, however, a conservative theme has persisted in the American experience, acting as "a stubborn dike to keep our liberalism from spilling over into radicalism."

Rossiter believes that the most important conservative principles at work in the American mind have been

traditionalism —reverence for the values inherited from the Founding Fathers

unity —belief that loyalty to common values should transcend particular interests

constitutionalism—belief that American rights are enshrined in the Constitution

religion —belief that democracy is strengthened because Americans believe in God

private property —belief that protection of private property is a cornerstone for all American rights.

Keeping these principles in mind, let us now consider Daniel Webster and Abraham Lincoln, two representatives of the conservatism in the American democratic mind.

Daniel Webster and National Conservatism

Not everyone admired Daniel Webster when he was alive, but everyone agreed that he was a man to be taken seriously. His champions among the Whigs, and especially the leading

merchants and industrialists in Boston, felt that Webster cast
a shadow as long as the Bunker Hill monument, and it was for
this reason, along with the fact that he served their interests
well, that they not only voted for Webster but subsidized him
as well. Even his bitterest enemies were impressed by Webster.
John Quincy Adams wrote about "the gigantic intellect, the
envious temper, the ravenous ambition, and the rotten heart
of Daniel Webster," and it was natural for Whittier, after
Webster's fateful seventh of March speech, to compare him
with the fallen Lucifer. For a long time Webster has played a
major role in all the important political histories of the United
States, but his importance to our intellectual history is sometimes overlooked. The consistent conservatism in his political
thought remains important, however, to any consideration of
the American democratic mind before the Civil War.

As a young schoolteacher in Maine in 1802, Webster wrote
to a friend that "the path to despotism leads through the mire
and dirt of uncontrolled democracy." If the American government ever fell, he warned, it would be through an administration
that subverted the conservative institutions of the Constitution in
the interests of "the sovereign people." Two years later, study-
ing law in Salisbury, New Hamphire, Webster was lamenting
over the political situation there. "The Federalists, as their manner is, set still and sigh at the depravity of the times. But sighs,
and tears and broken hearts are not worth a biscuit; they cannot
get a vote."

The two quotations from Webster's early letters suggest
a principle important in his later career. Webster came from
strong New England Federalist stock. He was deeply skeptical
of unchecked popular majorities, but he was also a practical
politician and recognized the futility of clinging to ideas which
had outlived their time. At the beginning of his political career
Webster opposed the two most important changes of the day.
He refused to support manufactures because he did not want
to see American farmers leave their peaceful flocks and fertile
fields for the "dust and smoke and steam" of the factory. He
opposed the popular election of state senators in the Massachusetts Constitutional Convention in 1820 because he felt that to

abandon the traditional apportionment of state senators on the basis of taxable wealth in a given district was to abandon the time-honored principle that political power follows property. Webster's ideas on both of these issues underwent significant modifications during the ensuing years. At the same time he never completely repudiated the principles that he first enunciated. This can be seen most easily by tracing his changing attitude toward industrialization. In 1814 it seemed to threaten the values he held most dear, all of which clustered around his vision of a nation of independent yeomen working their own lands. Ten years later Webster had moved from New Hampshire to Boston and his constituency showed a marked interest in manufactures. Webster began to sing the praises of steam. He rejoiced to discover that the American factory worker would not lose his identity in a proletariat class, but would work for wages, accumulate capital, and become a small capitalist himself. By the 1840's he was intoning the virtues of "this mighty agent, steam" in limiting the distinctions between rich and poor and raising up the masses "in the majesty of a common manhood."

In 1820 Webster had been staunchly against expanding the base of popular power in Massachusetts elections. As late as 1833 he was still warning of the dangers of too much democracy: "To be free the people must be intelligently free; to be substantially independent they must be able to secure themselves against want, by sobriety and industry; to be safe depositories of political power they must be able to comprehend and understand the general interests of the community, and must themselves have a stake in the welfare of that community."

Meanwhile the decline of the Federalist Party and Webster's intimate connections with the mill owners of Massachusetts was taking Webster into the Whig Party. By 1840 he was a strong contender for the presidential nomination, but along with Henry Clay was passed over for the more obscure William Henry Harrison. Whig strategy called for Van Buren, the Democratic candidate, to be attacked as an aristocrat while Harrison was to be celebrated as a representative of the common man. Coonskin democracy was to be overturned by coonskin whiggery, and Webster was called upon to play his part. He did his best, stumping the country and accusing the Democrats of pauperizing American labor by opposing the tariff and the bank. The editor of a Van Buren paper is supposed to have suggested that Harrison would be better off drinking hard cider in a log cabin than trying to make a career in the Capitol. Webster and the other campaign orators for the Whigs were quick to turn the alleged slur to their own advantage. The Jackson men, who tried to turn the poor against the rich, had now betrayed themselves by sneering at the humble life. "Witness the reproach against a candidate now before the people for their highest honors," Webster thundered, "that a log cabin, with plenty of hard cider, is good enough for him." Unfortunately Webster himself had not been born in a log cabin. His older brothers and sisters had been, however, and Webster exploited the fact every chance he got.

The contrast between Webster in 1820 and Webster in 1840 tells us a good deal about the problems faced by a conservative politician in the first half of the nineteenth century. The old-fashioned conservatism of the Federalists simply could not survive in an age when the most extravagant expectations of the people were constantly being surpassed. The new American democracy was working wonders and Webster knew it. He could not help but believe in the material advances of the people because the evidence was all around him. Nevertheless, his contributions to the rhetoric of 1840 were made more from a sense of party loyalty than from personal conviction, and he continued to insist on the importance of institutional restraints to the popular will. Like most conservatives he believed that organized religion was "the foundation of civil society," and when Stephen Girard, a wealthy Philadelphia merchant, left his inheritance for the purpose of founding an orphanage which would have excluded religious instruction, Webster, acting as counsel, undertook to break the will. He argued that an alleged charity which excluded religious teaching tended "to destroy the very foundation and framework of society," and could therefore not be considered a charity. In his conclusion Webster, in tones unmistakably reminiscent of Edmund Burke, insisted that Christianity was the law of the land.

Everything declared it. The massive cathedral of the Catholic; the Episcopalian church, with its lofty spire pointing heavenward; the plain temple of the Quaker; the log church of the hardy pioneer of the wilderness; the mementoes and memorials around and about us; the consecrated graveyards, their tombstones and epitaphs, their silent vaults, their mouldering contents; all attest it. *The dead prove it as well as the living.* The generations that are gone before speak to it, and pronounce it from the tomb. We feel it. All, all, proclaim that Christianity, general, tolerant Christianity, Christianity independent of sects and parties, that Christianity to which the sword and the fagot are unknown, general, tolerant Christianity, is the law of the land.

One of the most dramatic examples of popular democracy in American history took place in Rhode Island in 1841, when Thomas Dorr and his followers held a special constitutional convention for disenfranchised voters, framed a new constitution, and established their own government. For a while there were two governments in Rhode Island, one based on the old constitution derived from the royal charter, the other under Dorr's leadership claiming its legitimacy in the authority of the people. The Dorrites were put down by force, and Dorr himself went to prison. The legality of the Dorr government was decided by the Supreme Court in 1848. Webster defended the old government, and successfully attacked the legality of Dorr's action. He admitted that the Rhode Island constitution had been excessively restrictive regarding suffrage. If this was an error it was an error characteristic of prudent men acting in accordance with the best American tradition. The anarchy of Thomas Dorr was outside this tradition. The genius of the American political system, Webster said, was that the American people, in obedience to their "great conservative principle," deliberately protected themselves by constitutional restraints from "the sudden impulses of mere majorities."

Webster's most recent biographer, Richard Current, believes that the unifying principle in Webster's life and thought is "national conservatism." We have thus far discussed his conservatism in terms of a repeatedly stated fear of unchecked popular majorities, and an unwillingness to admit the blessings of industrialization until he had convinced himself that the American factory would turn wage-earners into capitalists and not create a mass of unpropertied (and therefore unreliable) citizens. We must now concern ourselves with his ideas about the American Union.

Nationalism is not of itself a conservative principle; carried to the extreme of a Mussolini or Hitler it becomes fanaticism. Webster's nationalism, however, was moderate. In a jingoistic age when many American politicians felt that our proper destiny was to extend American power everywhere in the Western hemisphere, Webster held that a nation based on principles of self-government could not continually absorb new territories and new cultures without threatening its own unity.

His nationalism derived in part from his Federalist background. His advocacy in the great cases *McCulloch* v. *Maryland* and *Gibbons* v. *Ogden* had been decisive in establishing the constitutional supremacy of the federal government over the states. To this legalistic nationalism, which he later called upon in his famous debates with Hayne and Calhoun, Webster added a romantic patriotism born partly of his memory of the past and partly of his vision for the future. Webster thought of the American Revolution as the action of a single people. "Let me indulge in refreshing remembrance of the past," he said to Hayne, "let me remind you that, in early times, no states cherished greater harmony . . . than Massachusetts and South Carolina. Would to God that harmony might again return! Shoulder to shoulder they went through the Revolution, hand in hand they stood round the administration of Washington, and felt his own great hand lean on them for support."

Webster felt that Americans were united, not only by the bonds of memory to a common past, but by self-interest. When he boasted that he stood "on a platform broad enough and firm enough to uphold every interest in the whole country," he was being sincere. He believed that the Whig program for tariffs, internal improvements, and a national bank would benefit every section. Union had been achieved, he recalled, "only by the discipline of our virtues in the severe school of adversity. It had its origin in the necessities of disordered finance, prostrate commerce and ruined credit." To Webster a canal in Ohio, a road over the Alleghenies, a railroad in South Carolina, benefited all the states: "In our contemplation, Carolina and Ohio are part of the same country. . . . We do not impose geographical limits to our patriotic feeling or regard; we do not follow rivers and mountains, and lines of latitude, to find boundaries, beyond which public improvements do not benefit us."

Finally, Webster believed that progress strengthened unity. The great agent of progress was steam, and the steam railroad was uniting "in metallic bands" all parts of the country. The railroad "joins the most remote regions and brings their inhabitants face to face, establishing a harmony of interests between them . . . the individual is sinking, and the mass rising up in the majesty of a common manhood."

No place on earth was more blessed than America, Webster said, and the reason was clear—that "copious fountain of national, social and personal happiness"—the federal union. If the Union was the source of all strength, prosperity, and virtue, it must be preserved at all cost. Here again Webster acted out the conservative role. He refused to speculate on how Americans could get along without Union. "I have not accustomed myself to hang over the precipice of disunion," he said, "to see, whether, with my short sight, I can fathom the depth of the abyss below . . . while the Union lasts, we have high, exciting, gratifying prospects spread out before us and our children. Beyond that I seek not to penetrate the veil. God grant that in my day, at least, that curtain may not rise."

The most difficult political decisions Webster had to make were on the slavery issue. How could he represent Massachusetts and still remain true to conservative principles? The tradition of antislavery sentiment in Massachusetts went back long before the abolitionists. Webster's opposition to the expansion of slavery was a matter of record. In the thirties he had clashed with Calhoun by holding that Congress did have the power to deal with slavery in the District of Columbia and should hear petitions on the subject.

When the conservative, interested above all in social unity, is forced to confront a divisive issue like slavery, highly charged with emotional and moral energy, he must find some middle ground solid enough to support all conflicting parties. By 1850 Webster could feel this ground giving way beneath his feet, as the controversy raged over the status of slavery in territory taken from Mexico. The South was determined that slavery should follow the flag. The abolitionists insisted that Americans who recognized a "higher law" could not let slavery expand, or support it by returning fugitive slaves. In the Senate the great triumvirate of Clay, Calhoun, and Webster debated the issue. Clay was for compromise. Calhoun was for secession, unless every Southern demand was met. Webster spoke on March 7 in what was probably his finest hour as a conservative. He pleaded for Americans to understand the causes of the problem. Slavery had existed at the time of the Constitution. The framers, not knowing how to eliminate the institution, had accepted it as a fact, but their willingness to abolish the slave trade indicated their confidence that slavery would die out in time. At the same time they gave the federal government no power to interfere with slavery within the states. With the invention of the cotton gin the situation had changed. Slavery became profitable, and Southerners now found it to their immediate self-interest to see it flourish. "The whole interest of the South became connected, more or less, with the extension of slavery." At the same time there developed in the North a growing body of opinion which held that slavery was morally wrong.

Webster attempted to show that each side had legitimate grievances. Northern sensibilities were injured when apologists for slavery attempted to prove that the free working man in the North was worse off than the plantation slave. On the other hand Southern interests were violated when Northerners refused to return fugitive slaves. The real villains were extremists in both parties who mistook "loud and violent talk for eloquence and reason."

The abolitionists had been nettling Webster for years, and he gave them special attention in his speech. Burke once accused the French philosophers of the Enlightenment of shaping their theories about natural rights into an underground mine that threatened to blow up "all examples of antiquity." Webster denounced the abolitionists in much the same tone: ". . . these persons are disposed to mount upon some particular duty as upon a war horse, and to drive furiously on and upon and over all other duties that may stand in the way. . . . They deal with morals as with mathematics; and they think what is right may be distinguished from what is wrong with the precision of an algebraic equation." Webster asked Americans to look at the world as it was. Slavery existed and was protected by law. Slaveholders also had their rights, including the enforcement of a fugitive slave law, and all citizens "not carried away by some fanatical idea" would respect those rights.

Webster's support made the Compromise of 1850 possible. The Union was preserved for another decade. Webster died in 1852, still hopeful, we may imagine, that a united America would continue to bear witness to what he called "the slow progress of moral causes in the improvement of mankind." Nine years later the horror began. Had he lived to see it Webster's one consolation might have been that another man of conservative principles, equally zealous in his love for the Union, was President when it happened.

Abraham Lincoln and Democratic Conservatism

Twenty years ago the eminent Lincoln scholar, J. G. Randall, published an essay entitled *Lincoln the Liberal Statesman*. The thesis of the essay was that since Lincoln embodied the classic values of the "American spirit" his career had to be considered in a "liberal framework." More recently Norman Graebner has taken up a contrary theme. "Lincoln maneuvered so that events found him in the right place," writes Graebner. "Seldom has a man who wielded power in such momentous times revealed such conservative habits of thought." A good case can be made for both positions. Lincoln was a liberal in the sense of being America's most eloquent champion of the democratic cause. To this extent he takes his place within the "liberal consensus" in American thought. To admit this, however, does not bring us very close to his unique qualities of mind. Lincoln was not a Jacksonian. He was not a reformer or agitator, and he shared Webster's nationalism but not his skepticism about popular government. His traditionalism, his religious sense, and his concern for unity, constitutionalism, and the rights of private property mark Lincoln as a spokesman for American democratic conservatism, and it is in this light that we must consider him.

Perhaps the best way to approach Lincoln as a representative of the American mind is to recall at the outset that he was a Western man and a politician. Frederick Jackson Turner wrote that Jackson's democracy was contentious and individualistic while Lincoln represented the more social side of frontier life, "the pioneer folk who entered the forest of the great Northwest to chop out a home, to build up their frontiers in the midst of a continually ascending industrial movement." Certainly the frontier environment made a lasting impact on Lincoln's mind. The fact that he was a product of the Southern stream of migration also left a mark. He grew up with people who had lived close to slavery, and he knew something about the depth of the white man's prejudice against the Negro. At the same time the informal manner and rough equality of Western society became a permanent part of his own personality. Finally the West helped to shape Lincoln's ideas about government; coming from a part of the country that needed roads, bridges, and canals, he early developed a conception of government that distinguished between the individual rights and collective needs of the people. "The legitimate object of government," he wrote once, "is to do for a community of people, whatever they need to have done, but cannot do *at all* or cannot *so well do,* for themselves in their separate and individual capacities."

The importance of the fact that Lincoln was a professional politician during most of his life should not be underestimated. Like other men in the same profession he was not above the use of sophistry. As a young Whig, for example, he defended the tariff on grounds that the only people hurt by it would be aristocrats living on imported European luxuries. Like other good politicians Lincoln tried to steer clear of divisive issues, and he successfully skirted the slavery issue in public until 1854. Lincoln was so adroit in tailoring what he had to say to the audience at hand that Stephen Douglas once accused him, with some justice, of taking a strong antislavery position when they appeared on platforms in northern Illinois, and an anti-abolitionist position in the southern part of the state. To these sound political instincts Lincoln added an expert knowledge of party organization, and Harry Carman and Reinhold Luthin have shown how much of his success in the White House can be attributed to his shrewd supervision of federal patronage.

T. Harry Williams has written that Lincoln represents "the supreme example in our history of the union of principle and pragmatism in politics." Reformers and reactionaries usually reflect a doctrinaire quality of mind. Lincoln's conservatism made him sensitive to the complexities of situations and wary of simple solutions. He was more an agent than a creator of political forces. Highly aware of the prevailing political winds of his own time, he knew how to tack and change direction in a shifting breeze, but his first purpose was always to keep the main thrust of his age behind him. Lincoln confessed as much himself when he said in 1864, "I claim not to have controlled events but confess plainly that events have controlled me."

No American has been more written about than Abraham Lincoln. Volumes have been devoted to his ideas on religion, his political philosophy, his legal career, his marriage, and his generalship, to name only a few of the aspects of his life that have been studied in detail. For the purposes of this discussion it will be convenient to consider three ideas fundamental to all his thinking: his belief in Providence; his belief in the dignity of free labor; his belief in the American mission.

In an age when American religious sentiment tended to be absorbed into evangelicalism, transcendentalism, or reform, Lincoln went his own way. Not metaphysical enough to be a transcendentalist, too much a man of reason to be converted, he was a man of great religious intensity who never joined a church. In 1846 when he was running for Congress against the Methodist minister Peter Cartwright, Lincoln was forced to reply to the charge that he did not subscribe to the tenets of Christianity. He admitted that he was not a church member, but said he had "never denied the truth of the Scriptures and . . . never spoken with intentional disrespect of religion in general, or of any denominations of Christians in particular." He went on to say that he could not, himself, support anyone for office who was an open enemy of religion. "Leaving the matter of eternal consequences between him and his Maker, I still do not think any man has the right thus to insult the feelings, and injure the morals, of the community in which he may live."

In a study of Lincoln's religious development William Wolf has shown how the loss of his son Willie and the awareness of the nation's suffering during the Civil War helped to shape Lincoln's early belief in determinism into a mystical faith in Divine Providence. Lincoln could not reconcile civil war with the existence of a supreme and benevolent God, except by assuming a divine purpose at work beyond human comprehension. "The Will of God prevails," he wrote (probably after the second Union defeat at Bull Run). "Both *may* be, and one *must* be wrong. God cannot be *for,* and *against* the same thing at the same time. In the present Civil War it is quite possible that God's purpose is something different from the purpose of either party. . . ."

Perhaps the most impressive thing about Lincoln was his ability to combine acute political sensitivity with profound moral insight. Amidst the tumult of war and political intrigue, assailed on every side more vituperatively than any other president, he retained his vision of the common guilt and tragedy of his countrymen. "The Almighty has His own purposes," he wrote in the Second Inaugural,

If we should suppose that American slavery is one of those offenses which, in the providence of God, must needs come, but which, having continued through His appointed time, He now wills to remove, and that He gives to both North and South, this terrible war, as the woe due to those by whom the offense came, shall we discern therein any departure from those divine attributes which the believers in a Living God always ascribe to Him? Fondly do we hope—fervently do we pray—that this mighty scourge of war may speedily pass away. Yet if God wills that it continue . . . as was said three thousand years ago, so still it must be said the judgments of the Lord are true and righteous altogether.

Daniel Webster had complained when Southerners made invidious comparisons between the welfare of slaves and the condition of the Northern working class. Lincoln also recognized this threat and gave a central place in his social and economic thinking to asserting the rights and dignity of the free American laborer.

The Southern argument, as put forth by men like George Fitzhugh, held that labor necessarily followed capital and that the slave system of labor was superior to free labor because slaves were well taken care of by their masters, while Northern capitalists exploited "free" workers, and left them at the mercy of the market so far as their subsistence or duration of employment were concerned. Lincoln spoke to this point in an address before the Wisconsin State Agricultural Society in 1859. He argued that labor was the source of capital and therefore superior to it. The Southern image of a fixed-wage earning class in the North was fallacious. "In these free states, a large majority are neither *hirers* nor *hired*. Men, with their families— wives sons and daughters—work for themselves; on their farms, in their houses and in their shops, taking the whole product to themselves, and asking no favors of capital on the one hand, nor of hirelings or slaves on the other." Most of those who did work for wages did so only long enough to build up a capital for themselves and begin their own enterprise. "If any continue through life in the condition of the hired laborer," Lincoln said, sounding very much like Benjamin Franklin, "it is not the fault of the system, but because of either a dependent nature which prefers it, or improvidence, folly, or singular misfortune."

Southerners argued that Negro slavery gave leisure to Southern gentlemen and thus contributed to gracious society in contrast to the competitive, capitalistic North where everyone was tied to the market place. Lincoln defended the North by pointing out that in the free states almost everyone was educated and almost everyone worked. He had grown up in the American Garden, and the image of the educated American yeoman, tilling his own fields "independent of crowned-kings, money-kings, and land-kings" was indispensable to his vision of America.

Lincoln's attitude toward the Negro and toward the institution of slavery was closely related to his conception of the dignity of free labor. During their debates together, Douglas kept trying to identify Lincoln as a believer in social equality for Negroes, and Lincoln always took conservative ground in denying the charge. "I have no purpose to introduce political and social equality between the white and the black races," he said. "There is a physical difference between the two, which in my judgment, will probably forever forbid their living together upon the footing of perfect equality, and inasmuch as it becomes a necessity that there must be a difference, I, as well as Judge Douglas, am in favor of the race to which I belong, having the superior position." If Lincoln's conception of the Negro was a far cry from that of Wendell Phillips, so was it also from the ideas of Fitzhugh or even Douglas. With all his limitations the Negro was still a man, entitled to all the natural rights enunciated in the Declaration of Independence. "I hold that he is as much entitled to these as the white man," Lincoln said. "I agree with Judge Douglas he is not my equal in many respects. . . . But in the right to eat the bread, without leave of anybody else, which his own hand earns, *he is my equal and the equal of Judge Douglas, and the equal of every living man.*"

Lincoln objected to slavery on moral grounds, but he also saw that the extension of slavery should be opposed as a threat to the dignity of free labor. He was in favor, he said, "of our new territories being in such a condition that white men may find a home. . . . I am in favor of this not merely . . . for our own people who are born amongst us, but as an outlet for *free white people everywhere,* the world over—in which Hans, and Baptiste and Patrick, and all other men from all the world, may find new homes and better their conditions in life."

When Lincoln was twenty-nine he spoke to the Young

Men's Lyceum in Springfield, Illinois, on "the perpetuation of our political institutions." He was fearful of the spread of mob law, he said, and apprehensive that an American dictator might be on the horizon. He attributed the decline in national virtue to the passing of the revolutionary generation. While they lived they were a living reminder of the principles on which the country was based. "They *were* the pillars of the temple of liberty, and now, that they have crumbled away, that temple must fall, unless we, their descendants, supply their places with other pillars. . . ." The conservative flavor of this passage, the sense of an honorable past now forgotten, of an American mission veering off its original course is repeated throughout Lincoln's writing.

Lincoln said that he "never had a feeling politically that did not spring from the Declaration of Independence." His devotion to the Union was not only a solemn constitutional obligation; it was primarily a devotion to the principles of the Declaration of Independence. The Union enshrined these principles for the world by promising "that in due time the weights should be lifted from the shoulders of all men, and that *all* should have an equal chance." This was the mission of America as Lincoln saw it, and when he visited Independence Hall on the way to his first inauguration he said he would "rather be assassinated on this spot than to surrender it."

Lincoln believed that if slavery was not wrong nothing was wrong, and he accused Douglas of "blowing out the moral lights around us" by refusing to take a position on the morality of the issue. Lincoln did not have the reformer's temperament, however, and he might never have been drawn into open debate on the subject had he not been convinced that the extension of slavery was a dangerous innovation which threatened to subvert the mission of America. Like Webster he argued that the Founding Fathers had accepted slavery only because they had to, that they had allowed it into the Union in the hope it would soon disappear. The Compromise of 1820 had been, Lincoln said, a reaffirmation of the original feeling that slavery must be contained. But in the 1850's all this was changed. A half century earlier Americans had tried to hide the institution the way a man "hides away a wen or a cancer, which he dares not cut out at once, lest he bleed to death." Now men claimed a sacred right not only to hold slaves but to take them anywhere in the Union. Lincoln mourned the erosion of traditional American values: "Little by little, but steadily as man's march to the grave, we have been giving up the OLD for the NEW faith. Nearly eighty years ago we began by declaring that all men are created equal; but now from that beginning we have run down to the other declaration, that for SOME men to enslave OTHERS is a 'sacred right of self-government.' " The American robe was soiled and trailed in the dust. Lincoln sought to conserve it in the spirit of the Revolution.

Believing as strongly as he did in the Declaration of Independence, Lincoln had to admit the right of revolution, but when the Southerners claimed secession as a revolutionary right, he said they were not justified. Their rights as a minority (especially the protection of slavery within the States) were guaranteed by the Constitution. So far as the disputes raging over the interpretation of the Constitution were concerned, Lincoln reminded his listeners in the First Inaugural Address that "no organic law can ever be framed with a provision specifically applicable to every question which may occur in practical administration." In such cases the majority had to prevail. The Declaration of Independence itself had said that governments should not be overturned "for light and transient causes," and Lincoln knew he did not depart from the principles of the American Revolution when he called secession "the essence of anarchy."

Believing that the Union of the states was perpetual and that the government had the right to maintain itself, Lincoln played a consistently conservative role in the Presidency. His conciliatory attitude toward the South, the refusal to disown the Fugitive Slave Law or to move against slavery in the states, the willingness to let the South strike the first blow, the generous terms he proposed for reconstruction all testify to his conservatism.

It was natural that the Wendell Phillipses of the world should have been distressed with Lincoln. They called him the "slave hound from Illinois" and castigated him for presiding over the greatest slaughter in history without clarifying the central moral issue—liberation of the Negro.

Lincoln saw the struggle in more comprehensive terms. At one point he went so far as to say that if he could save the Union without freeing a single slave he would do it. He could say this because he believed that to preserve the Union was to preserve the American mission, a mission that included all men everywhere and that would inevitably be extended to the Negro. The war, he said, was "essentially a people's contest" to conserve a government "whose leading object is to elevate the condition of men—to lift artificial weights from all shoulders; to clear the paths of laudable pursuit for all; to afford all an unfettered start, and a fair chance in the race of life . . . this is the leading object of the government for whose existence we contend."

FOUR

The Mind of the South

As American democracy expanded, so did the institution of
Negro slavery. As humanitarian and reform organizations proliferated in the North, political and social orthodoxy settled itself upon the South. On the surface, at least, it seemed as if
two conflicting civilizations, two conflicting minds, were developing. Our task in this chapter will be to separate those
ideas and values which the Southern mind shared with the
rest of America from those which were distinctively Southern,
and to pay special attention to the creative aspect of the Southern mind during the ante-bellum period.

THE DEMOCRATIC MIND
IN THE SOUTH

The Southern mind reflected a concern for individualism that was characteristic of American democracy. In his perceptive analysis *The Mind of the South,* Wilbur Cash claimed that the emphasis on individualism in the ante-bellum South was "perhaps the most intense the world has seen since the Italian Renaissance." He attributed this emphasis to the impact of the frontier and the plantation economy. The history of the South from 1800 to the Civil War, Cash claimed, was essentially "the history of the roll of frontier upon frontier—and on to the frontier beyond." This inhibited the development of class consciousness. The test of a man was not his name or where he came from, but what he could make of himself. The plantation, a self-contained center of power, reinforced the frontier influence. The society built around it was characterized by the absence of any central law-enforcing agency and by a distrust of outer authority, all of which contributed to the individualism of the average white Southerner.

The principle of equality was at work in the South as well as in the North, but for different reasons. Although the democratic ideas of the Jacksonians were prevalent in the South and many of the leading Southern political leaders learned their politics under Jackson, equality in the South was less a matter of philosophy than a matter of condition. The institution of slavery and the recognized inferiority of the Negro gave all white men membership in a dominant class. "No white man at the South serves another as a body servant," wrote the New Orleans journalist J. D. B. DeBow. "His blood revolts against this, and his necessities never drive him to it." What Wilbur Cash called a "peerage of white men," together with the more homogeneous population in the South, and the fact that in rural communities all the whites tended to be related to each other either by blood or close social ties, strengthened the democratic spirit fostered by the frontier and plantation.

We have previously noted that the American mind during

this period was religious but also deeply interested in science. In no part of the nation was religion more important than in the South. Originally a stronghold of Anglicanism, the Southern temperament had become increasingly attracted to the more evangelical message of Methodists, Baptists, and Presbyterians. By the time of the Civil War, a Protestantism that emphasized the infallibility of Scripture and the importance of conversion had become, along with slavery, part of the orthodox way of life in the South.

But the South also was interested in science. Southern colleges and universities introduced new courses in science during the period and lectures on scientific subjects aroused considerable public interest. When the great English geologist, Sir Charles Lyell, visited the South before the war, he was amazed at the number of people in obscure hamlets who were aware of his work and anxious to direct him to fossil remains in their particular neighborhoods. In men like Edmund Ruffin (scientific agriculture) and Matthew Maury (oceanography) Southerners could point to distinguished scientific investigators, and in places like Charleston and New Orleans they maintained substantial centers of scientific interest and research. Inevitably a major share of scientific energy in the South was drawn into the slavery controversy. Some of the people who tried to justify slavery on the basis of the racial inferiority of the Negro were no better than quacks. But there were others, like Josiah Nott and George Gliddon, who in seeking to prove the plural origin of races, as William Stanton has pointed out in *The Leopard's Spots,* gave their first loyalty to the spirit of scientific inquiry and made significant contributions to the infant science of anthropology in the pre-Darwinian period.

There are two aspects of the Southern mind that at first seem distinctive but can really be reconciled with the democracy that flourished elsewhere in America. The first is the image of the Southern "cavalier," the plantation aristocrat, the gentleman of grace and leisure who was alleged to be superior both in virtue and in talent to the coarse and grasping Yankee. In his challenging book, *Cavalier and Yankee,* William R. Taylor argues that the figure of the cavalier was a mythical creation that appealed to all Americans who were frightened by the pace and direction of social and economic change during the first half of the century. To many people, Taylor says, the aggressive, mercenary characteristics of the self-made man symbolized "both the restless mobility and the strident materialism of new world society" and challenged the existence of traditional American virtues. "They longed for a class of men immune to acquisitiveness, indifferent to social ambition and hostile to commercial life, cities, and secular progress."

Anxiety over the pace and direction of progress is a recurrent theme in American thought during this period. Jackson sought to restore the agrarian virtues of the old republic. Webster sought to transcend the divisive tendencies of his time with an appeal to nationalism. Lincoln believed that the American robe was trailing in the dust and he sought to repurify it in the spirit of the Revolution. Placed against this background the fiction of the Southern cavalier, shaped by serious Southern writers like John Pendleton Kennedy and popularized throughout the country in widely read magazines like *Godey's Lady's Book,* is not a regional phenomenon, but expresses a fundamental concern of the American democratic mind.

The second aspect of the Southern mind that appears irreconcilable with democracy is its refusal to entertain ideas critical of slavery. Yet the paradox presented by a society valuing individualism and equality but denying its members the right to criticize its basic institutional structure is more apparent than real. Southern orthodoxy on the slavery issue (and it was almost absolutely effective after 1837) is an extreme example of a common American tendency. Tocqueville and other observers have pointed out the danger of the tyranny of the majority in the American political system. This danger is always more threatening at the local than at the national level because, as Madison contended in his famous tenth *Federalist* paper, it is difficult to achieve a monolithic majority in a large, diversified nation. The self-contained land area, the homogeneous population, and the overwhelming importance of a single institution under attack from outside combined in the South to offer a perfect opportunity for the tyranny of the majority. A voice raised against slavery was stifled almost at the moment of speech. All of this is in striking contrast to the North where it sometimes seemed as if every man sought to raise his voice against every other man. There were perceptive thinkers in the North, however, men like Emerson, Thoreau, and Phillips, who could see in Northern democracy the same seeds of tyranny that had come to flourish in the South. The mobs that dragged Garrison to a Boston jailhouse and killed Elijah Lovejoy in Illinois were, after all, like the mobs that lynched abolitionists and free Negroes in the South, composed of democratic citizens and supported by democratic majorities.

The mind of the ante-bellum South possessed many characteristics common to the larger American mind, but it was also a thing apart. Although many sensitive thinkers during the period were disturbed by the spectacular rate of growth in the country, the prevalent American mood remained one of optimism. In the South, however, as C. Vann Woodward points out in *The Burden of Southern History,* the concern with justifying slavery tended to make people reject "such popular American ideas as the doctrine of human perfectibility, the belief that every evil has a cure, and the notion that every human problem has a solution. . . . In that most optimistic of centuries in the most optimistic part of the world, the South remained basically pessimistic in its social outlook and its moral philosophy."

To the pessimism which was rooted in the Southern mind we must add a remarkably militant temperament. Tocqueville said that the Southerner was convinced almost at birth "that he was born to command, and the first habit he contracts is that of ruling without resistance. His education tends then to give him the character of a haughty and hasty man,—irascible, violent, ardent in his desires, impatient of obstacles." John Hope Franklin's *The Militant South 1800-1861* documents in rich detail the accuracy of Tocqueville's insight by showing how the "martial spirit" of the region encouraged Southerners to develop skills in horsemanship and the use of arms, tolerate the custom of dueling, and support a system of military schools. Personal violence was accepted as a matter of course, and in some states, like Mississippi, it was "freely admitted in the 1850's that a man of talent seldom attained high political position if he had not demonstrated his manhood in some bloody affray."

The latent pessimism and violence in the Southern mind were tied to the existence of slavery. In a recent study, *The Mind of the Old South,* Clement Eaton analyzed the careers of fifteen representative Southerners in an attempt "to find a clue to the role of personality in a society that offered a far greater opportunity for personal influence than in the highly mechanized, impersonal society of America today." He could find no evidence that his subjects, or anyone else in the South, were "struggling with their consciences over the rightfulness of slavery," and he reluctantly concluded "that the history of the South in the thirty years preceding the Civil War . . . was largely a story of its representative men themselves being bent and warped by powerful economic and social forces."

In 1848 a merchant in Charleston, South Carolina, made the following entry in his journal: "A man selling birds in Broad Street made use of some expressions in regard to our domestic institution—was knocked down by Mr. George Walter and was then taken to the Police Office and he left here this afternoon in the Wilmington Boat." In 1856 a high school principal in Kentucky had his head shaved and his face varnished by a mob for writing a letter criticizing slavery to a friend in Ohio. The history of the South is full of incidents like these, but perhaps the greatest casualty of the slave system was not so much the violence it perpetrated on the persons of those who criticized it as the violence it worked on the intelligence of the capable, often brilliant, thinkers who tried to justify it.

THE SOUTHERN MIND AS APOLOGIST FOR SLAVERY

The proslavery argument, which absorbed so much of the intellectual energy of the South, can be divided into three parts—religious, racial, and philosophical. The religious argument was essentially a scriptural argument and probably the most important in the public mind. The careful exegesis of able biblical scholars like Thornton Stringfellow was intended to prove that slavery did not violate the letter of either the Old or New Testaments.

Expounders of the racial argument, like Josiah Nott and Samuel Cartwright, attempted to show that the Negro belonged to a separate and inferior race. Such biological and anthropological arguments, when combined with the denigration of Negro civilization outside slavery and the assertion that the Southern climate made manual labor difficult for white men, were intended to prove that Negro slavery was a natural institution.

The Southern intellectuals who attempted to defend slavery in terms of political and social philosophy have the most interest and relevance for us today. Thomas R. Dew's *Review of the Debate in the Virginia Legislature,* a defense of the Southern condition as it existed in 1832, when Virginia seriously considered abolishing slavery, is a good example of a kind of moderate conservatism which might have appealed to many people in the North. No responsible legislature, said Dew, "ever can legislate upon purely abstract principles, entirely independent of circumstances, without the ruin of the body politic." After showing the futility of colonization schemes and the economic impracticability of compensated emancipation, Dew concluded that, even if slavery were shown to be evil, there was no acceptable way of getting rid of it. His language re-echoed the rhetoric of Edmund Burke:

. . . if we cannot get rid of slavery without producing a greater injury to both the masters and slaves, there is no rule of conscience or revealed law of God which *can* condemn us. . . . The power of man has limits, and he should never attempt impossibilities. We do believe it is beyond the power of man to separate the elements of our population, even if it were desirable. . . . Let us reflect on these things, and learn wisdom from experience, and know that the relations of society, generated by the *lapse of ages,* cannot be altered in a *day.*

Twenty years later George Frederick Holmes made essentially the same point in a review of *Uncle Tom's Cabin* written for the *Southern Literary Messenger.* Holmes started out by claiming that even a Southern gentleman could not be expected to accord a "foul-mouthed **hag the same** deference that is rightfully due to the maiden purity of untainted innocence," but he soon took higher ground. He was willing to admit, he said, that the events related in the book could have happened, but when Mrs. Stowe argued that because slavery caused suffering it must be immediately abolished she was taking a position "absolutely fatal to all human society."

> It strikes at the very essence and existence of all community among men, it lays bare and roots up all the foundations of law, order and government. It is the very evangel of insubordination, sedition and anarchy. . . . In all periods of history—under all forms of government . . . instances of misery and barbarity equal to any depicted in this atrocious fiction, have been of constant recurrence. . . . But in all of them the real causes have been the innate frailties of humanity, the play of fortuitous circumstances, the native wickedness of particular individuals, and the inability of human wisdom or legislation to repress crime without incidentally ministering to certain vices.

Webster and Lincoln might have appreciated the cogency of arguments like those put forward by Dew and Holmes. But the Northern, democratic conservatives were forced to part company with the proslavery conservatives when the latter began to repudiate essential parts of the American tradition. When Southern thinkers found themselves forced to show that slavery was not a necessary evil but a positive good, when they abandoned conservatism for reaction, they isolated themselves from the rest of the American intellectual community. Thrown back upon themselves in their attempt to prove the superiority of slave society, they were forced to look at American institutions from a fresh perspective. The result has been described as an American "Reactionary Enlightenment." Its two most famous spokesmen were John C. Calhoun and George Fitzhugh.

John C. Calhoun

We have previously noticed that the two important formative influences on Lincoln were his Western background and his political temperament. Of the many forces that helped to shape the career and thought of John C. Calhoun, we might single out for particular attention the tremendous changes in America during the first half of the century, and the remarkably un-political temperament of Calhoun himself.

Calhoun was born in 1782, five years before the Constitution was written. He served in the federal government from 1810 to 1850 as congressman, cabinet member, vice-president, and senator. The unprecedented growth of the country during Calhoun's life and its implications for the South can be seen in terms of people and cotton. In 1790, when Calhoun was eight years old, the populations of North and South were approximately equal and the South was producing about five million pounds of cotton a year. In 1850 the South was producing almost one billion pounds of cotton a year, and the population of the North was almost half again as large as the South. Calhoun grew up with the South when that region became increasingly important economically and increasingly threatened with a diminution of political power. His whole political career can be seen as a response to this situation. Representing a minority interest, he attempted to retain for it at least an equal voice in the affairs of the federal government.

Harriet Martineau called Calhoun "the cast iron man who looks as if he had never been born, and could never be extinguished." In a country where successful politicians are supposed to be made of malleable stuff, Calhoun was notorious for his unbending attitudes, his rigid logic, his fondness for abstractions, and his insensitivity to personalities. Imbued with a Calvinistic sense of duty, he held that the purpose of life was to struggle against evil and that "to him who acts on proper principle, the reward is in the struggle more than in victory itself." Not even Thoreau or Phillips was more confident of his own vision of the right than Calhoun. "What I think I see," he wrote, "I see with so much apparent clearness as not to leave me a choice to pursue any other course, which has always given me the impression that I acted with the force of destiny."

Calhoun's first opportunity to act with the force of destiny came in 1828 when he drafted the *Exposition and Protest* for the South Carolinian legislature in response to the tariff act of the same year. The document was essentially a restatement of the states-rights doctrine earlier enunciated in the Virginia and

Kentucky Resolutions. Calhoun argued that the states had not abandoned their sovereignty by accepting the Constitution, and that they retained the right to refuse obedience to national acts that they judged unconstitutional. He claimed that the Congress, which possessed the power to impose duties on imports for revenue, had violated the Constitution by levying a discriminatory tariff favoring Northern industry at the expense of an agricultural South, which was forced to "sell *low*" in a world market and "buy *high*" in the domestic market. In 1832, acting on the principles stated in the *Exposition,* South Carolina called a convention for the purpose of adopting an ordinance nullifying the tariff of 1832. The state threatened to secede if the federal government attempted to enforce the tariff. The rest of the story is well known. President Jackson had a Force Bill passed authorizing the use of federal troops to enforce revenue collections. At the same time, at his urging, Congress brought in a tariff the next year with lower duties. Thereupon South Carolina repealed the Ordinance of Nullification and the crisis terminated.

Calhoun's theories on nullification aroused little interest elsewhere in the South and in the years that followed he began to think less in terms of the individual state as a check to national power and more in terms of the South as a region.

As a young man Calhoun had hoped that slavery would not last forever, that it might be "like the scaffolding of a building," and would be dismantled after it had served its purpose; but by the middle of the 1830's he was willing to defend the institution as a positive good. Margaret Coit has shown in her biography of Calhoun that his feeling about slavery, quite apart from his intellectual justification of it, was closely related to his own experience. His father had brought the first Negro slaves ever seen in the Carolina up-country. Calhoun had grown up with slaves and played with them as a boy. As a man he owned probably between thirty and ninety slaves. He bought them food, clothing, and medicine. His wife nursed them when they were sick. He gave them presents on special occasions, and sometimes he had them whipped. For Calhoun slavery was a way of life. He accepted the inferiority of the Negro as a fact, and assumed, as he once remarked to John Quincy Adams at the time of the Missouri Compromise, that the principles of the Declaration of Independence "are always understood as applying only to the white race."

His defense of the institution, however, was based more on social theory than on his own experience with a reasonably benevolent plantation system. While coping with a barrage of antislavery petitions in 1837 and 1838, Calhoun attempted to make his colleagues in the Senate see that "there never has yet existed a wealthy and civilized society in which one portion of the community did not, in point of fact, live on the labor of the other." The great blessing of the South, secured by "a mysterious Providence" which "brought together two races from different parts of the globe" was that the inferior Negro was suited by nature to labor for the white man. The result was that in the North, as in Europe, the exploitation of labor by capital resulted in class conflict and violence, whereas harmony reigned in the South. Although Calhoun's social analysis seems to anticipate Marx's conception of class struggle, his purpose was to encourage conservatism. He argued that slavery was a positive good to the North as well as the South because it exerted a stabilizing influence on all American society.

> The blessing of this state of things extends beyond the limits of the South. It makes that section the balance of the system, the great Conservative power, which prevents other portions, less fortunately constituted, from rushing into conflict. In this tendency to conflict in the North between labor and capital, which is constantly on the increase, the weight of the South has and will ever be found on the Conservative side; against the aggression of one or the other side, which ever may tend to disturb the equilibrium of our political system.

The conservative coalition between Southern agriculture and Northern business interests, which Calhoun desired, and which has played such an important part in our political life in the twentieth century, disappointed Calhoun in his own lifetime. Losing faith in the possibility of a political resolution to sectional antagonisms under the existing framework of government, Calhoun placed his last hope in the willingness of Americans to make fundamental changes in their Constitution in order to avert disaster.

Calhoun's masterpiece, the *Disquisition on Government,* was written in the 1840's but was not published until after his death. It is based on a dual theory of human nature. Calhoun assumes that man is motivated by social instincts and by self-interest. Because his instincts to self-interest are more powerful than his social instincts "government is necessary to the existence of society." Government does not arise out of a social contract. It is as natural as society and exists to protect men from each other and thus to preserve the race. Since man's essential nature is not changed by his participation in government, the problem for theorists and legislators is to assure that political power is administered for the good of the whole people and not in the self-interest of a part of the people. The Constitution is the device by which men attempt to accomplish this goal. "Constitution," Calhoun writes, "is the contrivance of man, while government is of divine ordination. Man is left to perfect what the wisdom of the Infinite ordained as necessary to preserve the race."

The whole art and science of government, Calhoun believed, should be directed toward creating a good constitution. The first principle to be observed is to give to the people who are ruled the power to resist their rulers, which means giving them the right of suffrage, "the indispensable and primary principle in the *foundation* of a constitutional government."

The establishment of suffrage by itself, however, is no panacea. The problem is transferred from the rulers to the people, and the necessity now is to find a way to keep the majority from tyrannizing over the minority. If the whole community had identical interests so that any government action that damaged one part also damaged every other part, the right to suffrage might be sufficient. But such is not the case, and the existence of diverse interests within the community makes it inevitable that particular actions of elected governments will benefit some parts of the community at the expense of others. Calhoun illustrated this in terms of the fiscal action of a government. Any system of taxation and disbursement, he said, always favors some interests at the expense of others.

What the one takes from the community under the name of taxes is transferred to the portion of the community who are the recipients under the name of disbursements. But as the recipients constitute only a portion of the community, it follows, taking the two parts of the fiscal process together, that its action must be un- equal between the payers of the taxes and the recipients of their proceeds. Nor can it be otherwise; unless what is collected from each individual in the shape of taxes shall be returned to him in that of disbursements, which would make the process nugatory and absurd.

The only way to protect the minority, argued Calhoun, is to give it some kind of controlling voice in legislative matters that concern itself. This is the famous "concurrent majority." Calhoun proposed that each major interest or section in the country have the right to veto any action of the numerical ma- jority when a majority within that section find the act hostile to its own interests. The result, Calhoun believed, will enforce compromise and ensure harmony.

. . . By giving to each interest, or portion, the power of self-pro- tection, all strife and struggle between them for ascendancy is pre- vented; and thereby, not only every feeling calculated to weaken the attachment to the whole is suppressed, but the individual and social feelings are made to unite in one common devotion to country. Each sees and feels that it can best promote its own prosperity by conciliating the good will and promoting the prosperity of the others.

His political philosophy was partly the result of his own fondness for logical speculation, but it was also a product of his political experience. When Calhoun was five years old James Madison had written in *Federalist Paper Number 10* that the diversity and size of the United States would prevent the develop- ment of a factional majority capable of tyrannizing over the minority. Calhoun believed that his own experience showed Madison to be wrong. His mistake had been in underestimating the pull of power and the rewards to be gained by the victorious party in a national election. Calhoun spelled this out in a speech to his constituents in 1847. In analyzing Northern opinion regarding slavery he estimated that 5 per cent of the people were abolitionists, another 5 per cent were proslavery, while the single largest group of about 70 per cent disapproved of slavery but felt that nothing could be done about it. The final group, about 20 per cent, consisted of "the political leaders of the respective parties and their partizans and followers." Calhoun contended that since political power in most of the Northern states was evenly balanced, the abolitionists were courted by both major parties, and thus exerted an influence far greater than their numbers.

The main cause or motive, then, of this crusade against our domestic institutions, is to be traced to the all-absorbing interest which both parties take, in carrying the elections, especially the Presidential. Indeed, when we reflect that the expenditure of the Federal Government, at all times great, is now swelled probably to seventy millions of dollars annually, and that the influence of its patronage gives it great sway . . . it is not at all surprising that both parties should take such absorbing interest in the Presidential election. . . . In such a state of things, it is not a matter for wonder, that a course of policy, so well calculated to conciliate a party like the abolitionists, as that of excluding slavery from the territories, should be eagerly embraced by both parties in the non-slaveholding states.

Under existing conditions the militancy and increasing power of antislavery zealots in the North could only be countered by the increased militancy of slavery's defenders in the South. Calhoun played this role out in the Senate, savagely and defiantly, during the last years of his life. He sought union, not secession, but a union in which slavery would be permanently guaranteed no matter what the ratio of free to slave states. The only salvation, he believed, was for Americans to incorporate the principle of the concurrent majority into their federal institutions.

George Fitzhugh

Fitzhugh was born in Prince William County, Virginia, in 1806, and lived most of his life on a nondescript plantation in

Port Royal. He was largely self-educated, occasionally practiced law, and served as a clerk in the Attorney General's office before the war, and as an associate judge of the Freedmen's Court after the war. Essentially, however, Fitzhugh was a journalist who from 1854 to 1867 published over a hundred articles in Southern journals like the *Richmond Enquirer* and *DeBow's Review*. In addition he wrote two important books, *Sociology for the South, or the Failure of Free Society,* (1854) and *Cannibals All! or Slaves Without Masters* (1856).

Fitzhugh is a thinker who resists easy definitions. C. Vann Woodward, in his introduction to a recent edition of *Cannibals All,* points out that he cannot be fitted into the convenient stereotypes usually associated with proslavery writers. He was not an agrarian, not a feudalist, not a racist. He was, curiously enough, a man, like Phillips and Garrison, whose cheerful disposition was belied by the ferocity of his prose. Fitzhugh is the only other proslavery thinker who approaches Calhoun in stature. His style, however, is entirely different. Where Calhoun is logical, dispassionate, and legalistic, Fitzhugh is intuitive and emotional. Although far from being a transcendentalist, he frequently writes like one, as if he sought like Emerson "to affront and reprimand the smooth mediocrity and squalid contentment of the times." At the risk, therefore, of making Fitzhugh appear more of a systematic thinker than he actually was, let us consider his ideas under three basic categories: his criticism of free society; his attitude toward progress; his defense of slavery.

Fitzhugh's attack on free society was essentially an attack on the laissez-faire philosophy. "Liberty and equality are new things under the sun," he proclaimed, "and we have conclusive proof that liberty and equality have not conduced to enhance the comfort or the happiness of the people." Fitzhugh argued that a government based on the principle of free competition was only legalized war and exploitation. Government exists to protect people from each other; free competition looses them at each others' throats, and is "that war or conflict to which Nature impels her creatures, and which government was intended to restrict." Fitzhugh contended that "equality of rights" meant "giving license to the strong to oppress the weak." Astute and avaricious men were left free to exploit their less favored neighbors. The result was a society supported by the unrewarded toil of simple-minded, strong-bodied workers. Fitzhugh spelled this out in passages that sound very much like Marx.

They bear the whole weight of society on their shoulders; they are the producers and artificers of all the necessaries, the comforts, the luxuries, the pomp and splendor of the world; they create it all and enjoy none of it; they are the muzzled ox that treadeth out the straw; they are at constant war with those above them, asking higher wages but getting lower; for they are also at war with each other, underbidding to get employment. This process of under-bidding never ceases so long as employers want profits or laborers want employment. It ends, when wages are reduced too low to afford subsistence, in filling poor houses, and jails, and graves.

Fitzhugh's attack on capitalism was as violent as any socialist's. In *Cannibals All,* he actually used many of the same sources that Marx would use ten years later in *Capital,* to demonstrate the dehumanizing tendencies of "free competition" on child and female labor. Nor did he content himself only with pointing out the physical effects of capitalism—the unemployment, poverty, and vice—he also indicted it for its psychological consequences. In a capitalistic society that put material gain as the end of life, one man's success was marked by another's failure; fortunes shifted rapidly, with the result that the human personality was haunted by insecurity, anxiety, and unhappiness.

Jefferson had said that government is best which governs least. Fitzhugh entitled one of his chapters "The world is too little governed." He believed that positive government support was necessary to build up manufactures, transportation facilities, and cities in the South. Thus his criticism of the North was not levied against industrialization but against an industrialized society based on free labor.

Fitzhugh thought that the revolutions of 1848 and 1849 in Europe were clear evidence that free society was destroying itself. He was sympathetic with the socialists' analysis of the evils of capitalism, and for their concern for the weaker, unprotected members of society, but he rejected the socialist solution as being contrary to the principles of human nature. "The attempt to establish government on purely theoretical abstract speculation, regardless of circumstance and experience, has always failed," he said, "never more signally than with the Socialists." The socialists talked of a society in which everyone lived together in harmony and equality, forgetting that "every social structure must have its substratum." The South, unharried by notions of freedom and equality, reconciled substratum with harmony by working Negro slaves.

Fitzhugh was one of the few Americans of his day who did not believe in progress. Except in science and technology, he claimed, the world had actually been retrogressing. The result was that men had more things to tinker with and could travel a good deal faster, but in a moral sense civilization had not improved at all. The history of the modern mind was the history of retrogression. It started at the time of the Reformation when, in the interest of a fictitious "right of private judgment," the powers of the church ("the noblest charity fund in the world") were weakened, and the poor were left naked before the rise of an exploiting middle class. The Revolution of 1688 in England worked the same effect by weakening the aristocracy and crown, "the natural friends, allies and guardians of the laboring class." The great example of folly in the history of the modern mind was the Enlightenment, and the two leading philosophical villains were John Locke and his disciple Thomas Jefferson. Knowing that Jefferson's ideas and their enshrinement in the Declaration of Independence inspired abolitionists in the North and inhibited timid souls in the South, Fitzhugh argued that Jefferson's principles were at war not only with slavery but with "all government, all subordination, all order." The only philosophy of natural rights that made sense, Fitzhugh said, was one that recognized the rights of masters to hold slaves.

The order and subordination observable in the physical, animal and human world show that some are formed for higher, others for lower stations—the few to command, the many to obey. We conclude that about nineteen out of every twenty individuals have a "natural and unalienable right" to be taken care of and protected . . . in other words they have a natural and unalienable right to be slaves. The one in twenty are as clearly born or educated or some way fitted for command and liberty. Not to make them rulers or masters is as great a violation of natural right as not to make slaves of the mass.

The trouble with Jefferson, Fitzhugh thought, was that he was blind to the world around him. Alexander Pope may have been excessively conservative when he said "whatever is, is right," but he was on incalculably sounder ground than Jefferson, who seemed to believe "whatever is, is wrong."

Although Fitzhugh did not believe in progress, he did recognize the inevitability of change. He distinguished between the kind of revolutionary change based on the abstract ideas of individuals and the kind of social change that was "the thought and act of society." Fitzhugh believed in the infallibility of society. "Its harmony is its health," he said, "and to differ with it is heresy or treason. . . ." Fitzhugh, like most conservatives, was an organicist. "The social body," he said, "is of itself a thinking, acting, sentient being." The genius of the American Revolution was that it had been a social movement, "and had nothing more to do with philosophy than the weaning of a calf. It was the act of a people seeking national independence, not the Utopian scheme of speculative philosophy seeking to establish human equality and social perfection."

Edmund Burke once said that if he were forced to choose between truth and peace he would always choose peace. If Fitzhugh had ever been asked to choose between reason and institutions he would always have chosen institutions, for they made up the fabric of society. "State governments, and senators, and representatives and militia," he wrote, "and cities and churches and colleges and universities, and landed property are institutions. Things of flesh and blood, that know their rights, 'and knowing dare maintain them.' We would cherish them. They will give permanence to government, and security to State Rights."

In defending slavery Fitzhugh proceeded on the assumption that the best defense was a good offense. In his view the most telling point to be made about free society (and he tried to put this in dozens of different ways) was its immorality. "The moral effect of free society," he wrote, "is to banish Christian virtue, that virtue which bids us love our neighbor as ourself, and to substitute the very equivocal virtues proceeding from mere selfishness." The only remedy for this evil was "to identify the interests of the weak and the strong, the poor and the rich." Slavery did just that. A plantation, Fitzhugh said, was "the beau ideal of Communism," in which the worker "in old age and in infancy, in sickness and in health" was rewarded, "not according to his labor, but according to his wants."

A favorite argument of the abolitionists was that slavery degraded the master. The example of fugitive slaves, incidents of brutality on the part of some masters, and the high rate of miscegenation were cited as evidence. Fitzhugh believed that the complete dependence of the slave encouraged love, not vice. "A state of dependence is the only condition," he said, "in which reciprocal affection can exist among human beings." No wonder that the slaveholder was a man of high moral character. "His whole life is spent in providing for the minutest wants of others. . . . Hence he is the least selfish of men. . . . Is not the head of a large family almost always kind and benevolent? And is not the slaveholder the head of the largest family? Nature compels master and slave to be friends; nature makes employers and free laborers enemies."

The mention of family brings us to a final point in Fitzhugh's defense of slavery. Although he thought very little of John Locke, Fitzhugh held a high opinion of Locke's now forgotten adversary, Sir Robert Filmer, a seventeenth century monarchist and staunch proponent of patriarchal authority. Filmer had contended that the family unit was the basis of political society and that patriarchal authority was the source of political authority. The argument made more than one hundred fifty years earlier seemed very close to the Southern experience. Throughout most of the South the plantation, an extended family, with the slaveholder reigning at the head, was the basic unit of social organization. The Southern planter, Fitzhugh said, was a patriarch, and his authority over wife, children, and slaves was a part of the natural order. The Virginia patriarchs who had made the most difference on American history, men like

Jefferson and Madison, claimed Locke as their intellectual father. Fitzhugh, a patriarch valiant in lost causes, was proud to acknowledge Sir Robert Filmer.

THE REACTIONARY ENLIGHTENMENT

Louis Hartz in *The Liberal Tradition in America* compares Southern thinkers like Fitzhugh and Calhoun to the philosophers of the French Enlightenment in their "sheer passion to shock, to tear down ancient idols, to stick pins in the national complacency." He describes the mind of the ante-bellum South as "the great imaginative moment in American political thought, the moment when America almost got out of itself and looked with some objectivity on the liberal formula it has known since birth."

Hartz also points out the difficulty Calhoun and Fitzhugh had in trying to be consistent reactionaries. Calhoun's constitutionalism is imbued with the spirit of John Locke, and his concurrent majority is the kind of rational contrivance that Burke would have abhorred. Calhoun's problem, as Hartz says, was how to be authentically conservative in a society which is traditionally liberal. The problem was too much, even for his logical mind. Fitzhugh's attack on Locke and economic individualism puts him more clearly in the reactionary camp. But even he slips into the mainstream of American thought on occasion. In his indictment of capitalism, for example, he sounds as humanitarian as any Northern reformer. And for all his rhetorical raving about inequality, Fitzhugh still finds occasion to justify the South in terms of the "liberty and equality" of her white population.

Certainly Fitzhugh was a perceptive critic of life in the North. After the war Northern reformers, including Wendell Phillips, would make many of his same points. But Fitzhugh's task, like Calhoun's, was a hopeless one. The difference between a radical like Phillips and a radical like Fitzhugh is that Phillips had the American tradition behind him. The majority may not have agreed with Phillips but they had to take him seriously.

Fitzhugh cut himself off from the American past, and was ignored.

Despite the lasting value of what Calhoun had to say about the necessity of compromise in America and the sharpness of Fitzhugh's analysis of American materialism, one cannot help but feel that these men might have played a greater role. Fitzhugh once admitted that he saw "great evils in slavery," but he was not prepared to write about them. If there was one thing the South needed, saddled as it was in a new democracy, with one of the most severe slave codes the world had ever known, it was self-criticism. The Negroes have not been the only slaves in the South. Like communist intellectuals, whom they resemble in so many ways, Calhoun and Fitzhugh could only be effective in criticizing another society. When they looked at their own they were mute.

FIVE

The Democratic
Imagination

Americans won their political independence from Great Britain in the Revolution and confirmed it in the War of 1812. Political independence was one thing, however, and cultural independence was another. In 1820 Americans were still buying seven English books for every three American ones. As national feeling grew stronger, numerous pleas were made for the development of a distinctively American literature, but American poetry and fiction remained largely derivative. Until Washington Irving and James Fenimore Cooper appeared, English critics could still sneer at the incongruity of any one reading "an American book,"

94

and even Irving was much more a "man of letters" in the Old World sense than a spokesman for American culture.

Oliver Wendell Holmes said that Emerson's Phi Beta Kappa address at Harvard in 1837 was an American "intellectual Declaration of Independence." Entitling his address "The American Scholar," Emerson announced that the time was come "when the sluggard intellect of this continent will look from under its iron lids and fill the postponed expectation of the world with something better than the exertions of mechanical skill. Our day of dependence, our long apprenticeship to the learning of other lands draws to a close. The millions that around us are rushing into life cannot always be fed on the sere remains of foreign harvests. Events, actions arise, that must be sung, that will sing themselves." The American experience encouraged the development of self-trust, optimism, and pride. Emerson provided metaphysical support for these qualities when he insisted that the American scholar must not become "a mere thinker, or still worse, the parrot of other men's thinking" but *"Man Thinking."* He must recognize the genius of his own inspiration and be true to it, be willing to learn from nature without becoming a collector of information, knowledgeable in books without becoming a book worm. "Man thinking must not be subdued by his instruments. Books are for the scholar's idle time. When he can read God directly, the hour is too precious to be wasted in other mens' transcripts of their readings."

A common complaint of writers and artists in early nineteenth century America was the difficulty of creating an indigenous literature in a nation with such a short history. Emerson's rejoinder was that the American scholar must be present-minded, willing to concern himself with that most characteristic American phenomenon—the ordinary man immersed in the ordinary business of life. "I ask not for the great, the remote, the romantic. . . . I embrace the common, I explore and sit at the feet of the familiar, the low. Give me insight into today, and you may have the antique and future worlds. What would we really know the meaning of? The meal in the firkin; the milk in the pan; the ballad in the street; the news of the boat; the glance of the eye; the form and the gait of the body. . . ."

Emerson was calling for the poet of democracy. He sought to heed that call himself, but his own style and temperament fitted him more to the essay. His influence on Whitman, however, as we shall see, was profound. In this sense, as the prophet for a new generation of American scholars, Emerson was the most influential intellectual of his time. Others had made similar pleas before him. In an authoritative study *The Quest for Nationality,* Benjamin Spencer points out that Emerson's address was "the most brilliant link in a long chain of academic discourses relating literature and national welfare." Emerson's voice was decisive in stirring the American imagination. If he had helped to launch the careers of only Thoreau and Whitman, his impact on the shaping of American literature would be of the highest importance. As we shall see, however, his influence on writers who disagreed with him, like Hawthorne and Melville, was equally important. Emerson's ideas about God, man, nature, and art, formalized to some extent in the movement we know as New England Transcendentalism, acted, as David Bowers writes in *The Literary History of the United States,* "as a kind of model and repository of ideas from which American, in particular New England, writers could borrow in their self-imposed task of creating a new metaphysics for democracy out of the theological and intellectual materials of the American past."

The history of American literature has been rewritten during the past quarter of a century. Our earliest literary historians tended to emphasize the derivative aspect of American literature. They described the transplanting of English prose and poetry in the new world. A second group of historians, active in the first three decades of this century, emphasized the American quality of our literature, but concentrated almost exclusively on political, economic, and social thought. Vernon Parrington's *Main Currents in American Thought* is the best and most influential example. An important shift in emphasis can be observed with the publication of F. O. Matthiessen's *American Renaissance* in 1941. Whereas Parrington had confessed that he was interested in American writers as thinkers rather than artists, Matthiessen indicated that his main concern would be to analyze the achievement of the classic American writers in terms of the literary imagination. Matthiessen had previously published a critical analysis of T. S. Eliot, and his study of Emerson, Thoreau, Hawthorne, Melville, and Whitman was a close examination of the conceptions held by these writers "concerning the function and nature of literature, and the degree to which their practice bore out their theories."

The concern with our major writers as artists, officially recognized by the publication of the *Literary History of the United States* in 1948, has forced us to revise our thinking about the American mind. The older view had been that each of our important writers reflected important ideas in the American experience in a fairly straightforward way and that most of them could be categorized as liberals or conservatives, optimists or pessimists. The current tendency is to see them as major artists capable of containing within themselves, and expressing in their art, the major contradictions of their age. "They are 'purer' artists than their European contemporaries," writes Richard Chase in a recent essay, "and they transmute the contradictions of their society into the aesthetic properties of their writing rather than report social realities or make intellectual formulations." Keeping this in mind let us now turn our attention to the work of Whitman, Cooper, Hawthorne, and Melville.

WHITMAN: THE DEMOCRAT AS POET

Walt Whitman's life almost spanned the century. He was born just seven years after the war of 1812 and died in 1892, one year before Frederick Jackson Turner wrote his famous essay announcing the close of the frontier and its influence on American history.

Whitman's expansiveness, his intense individualism, and ardent democracy can be explained in part by family background. He was born on a Long Island farm in a household where self-reliance and democratic radicalism were already entrenched. His father was a man of vigorous, independent intellect who liked to work with his hands, vote for Democrats of the Jefferson-Jackson stripe, and follow the kind of avant garde reform causes espoused by Frances Wright. Young Walt could trace Dutch, English, Quaker, Yankee, and Calvinist strains in his ancestry. Perhaps the most important was Quakerism. Although he never formally became a Quaker, he was impressed by the doctrine of the Inner Light, and this helped to support his own self-assurance in later life.

Of all the formative influences on Whitman before the publication of *Leaves of Grass,* none was more important than his career as a political journalist. Whitman never had much of a formal education. He got his first job in a newspaper office at the age of twelve, and for the next thirty-four years, in an itinerant career which perfectly illustrates the social mobility of nineteenth century Americans, divided his time between journalism, schoolteaching, and carpentry. He was successful enough as a journalist to serve as editor of the Brooklyn *Daily Eagle* from 1846 to 1848. The *Eagle* was a prominent Democratic paper, and at this time Whitman was almost as much a professional politician as a journalist. The experience of editing a major paper in one of the largest American cities during a period when it was growing spectacularly left its mark on him. Few men have ever been more suited for the job and the place than Whitman. He loved the swarming city, always in motion with its crowded omnibuses and ferries (he knew the drivers and the pilots by name). He rejoiced equally in the thronging immigrants and in the famous public figures he encountered in the streets. Webster, Clay, Jackson, Van Buren, Seward, Lincoln—he saw them all at one time or another in New York. The city, with its frenzied activity and the great bay alongside, symbolized the vitality and expansiveness of America. And when his own nature called for a change of rhythm, there were always the peaceful meadows and solitary beaches of Long Island.

Beside Whitman the empathetic reporter we must put Whitman the partisan Democrat, who in the *Eagle* supported humanitarian causes, condemned conservatives as "pestilential to our party," and upheld the dignity of American culture. "Give us American plays," he wrote on one occasion, "fitted to American opinions and institutions. . . . The drama of this country *can* be the mouthpiece of freedom. . . . It can wield potent sway to destroy any attempt at despotism."

We know that even as he wrote these words Whitman was groping in his notebook for a new kind of language which might carry a new kind of message. When his opposition to slavery brought him into conflict with the Democratic Party in 1849 and interrupted his journalistic career, Whitman was able to spend more time on his notebooks. In 1855, having set the type with his own hands, he published the first edition of *Leaves of Grass*.

Leaves of Grass was Whitman's supreme achievement. He revised it many times throughout his life, and it cannot be said to have been finished until he died. His preface to the first edition, however, is probably the clearest statement he made anywhere of what he was trying to do. Many readers found the preface as obscure as the poem, but to others it must have seemed as if the author was the very embodiment of Emerson's American scholar. "The United States themselves," Whitman announced, "are essentially the greatest poem." The American poet, therefore, would have to be "commensurate" with the people and their land. Log cabins, trappers, ferrymen, mountains, lakes, rivers, mechanics, fisherman, slaves, abolitionists—all of this and infinitely more would make up what Whitman called "the great psalm of the republic." For such poetry the expression of the American poet would have to be "transcendent and new."

In his preface Whitman enumerates specific virtues that the American poet must acknowledge and express. The first is faith, which he calls "the antiseptic of the soul . . . it pervades the common people and preserves them. . . . They never give up believing and expecting and trusting. There is that indescribable freshness and unconsciousness about an illiterate person that humbles and mocks the power of the noblest expressive genius. The poet sees for a certainty how one not a great artist may be just as sacred and perfect as the greatest artist."

A second virtue is self-trust, reconciling individual dignity with service to others. "This is what you shall do: Love the earth and sun and the animals, despise riches, give alms to everyone that asks, stand up for the stupid and the crazy, devote your income and labor to others, hate tyrants, argue not concerning God, have patience and indulgence toward the people, take off your hat to nothing known or to any man or number of men."

A third virtue is belief in liberty. "Liberty is poorly served by men whose good intent is quelled from one failure or two failures or any number of failures, or from the casual indifference or ingratitude of the people. . . . Liberty relies upon itself, invites no one, promises nothing, sits in calmness and light, is positive and composed and knows no discouragement."

A fourth virtue is naturalness. The American poet will find nothing American that is not also natural. "These American States strong and healthy and accomplished shall receive no pleasure from violations of natural models and must not permit them. . . . To put upon cornices or monuments or on the prows or sterns of ships, or to put anywhere before the human eye indoors or out, that which distorts honest shapes or which creates unearthly beings or places or contingencies is a nuisance and a revolt."

The central poem out of which all the rest of *Leaves of Grass* grew is "Song of Myself." The characteristics of the poem that help us to locate Whitman's position with respect to the transcendentalists are immediately obvious. The first three lines echo Emerson.

> I celebrate myself, and sing myself
> And what I assume you shall assume
> For every atom belonging to me as good belongs to you.

The apparent egocentricity of these lines hardly overreached Emerson's own words. Emerson had said that this was the age of the first person singular, and he must have agreed when Whitman identified the first person singular not only with himself as poet but also with the whole American democracy. The lines

> Of every hue and caste am I, of every rank and religion
> A farmer, mechanic, artist, gentleman, sailor, quaker
> Prisoner, fancy-man, rowdy, lawyer, **physician**, priest

reflect Emerson's belief in the spiritual unity of all men. Emerson's sense of fraternity may have been a good deal chillier than Whitman's but it was no less sincere.

Many critics objected to Whitman's poetry because of its formlessness. Compared to Longfellow's finished rhymes, Whitman's lines seemed rough and clumsy.

> What blurt is this about virtue and about vice
> Evil propels me and reform of evil propels me, I
>   stand indifferent
> My gait is no fault-finder's or rejecter's gait,
> I moisten the roots of all that has grown.

Whitman believed that the "expression of the American poet" had to be "transcendent and new." Here again we notice a resemblance to Emerson, who believed that the form was less important than the idea of a poem, and that the poet was less a craftsman than a vessel through which inspiration passed. "For it is not metres," Emerson said, "but a metre-making argument that makes a poem—a thought so passionate and alive, that, like the spirit of a plant or an animal, it has an architecture of its own, and adorns nature with a new thing. . . ."

The passages in the poem that made Emerson flinch were a product of Whitman's sensuous imagination. He thought of himself as "the poet of the body" as well as "the poet of the soul" and acted upon the belief in lines like the following:

> Divine am I inside and out, and I make holy whatever
>   I touch or am touched from
> The scent of these arm-pits aroma finer than prayer
> This head more than churches, bibles and all the creeds.

Emerson, who loved nature but constantly strove to transcend the experience of the senses, would never be able to understand Whitman's belief that in America the body should be as free as the soul. Indeed he hardly knew how to describe Whitman's emphasis on sexual imagery, and once wrote to a friend about "our wild Whitman, with real inspiration but choked by titanic abdomen."

Whitman confessed his debt to Emerson by saying, "I was simmering, simmering, simmering; Emerson brought me to a boil." When he sent Emerson a copy of the first edition of *Leaves of Grass,* the latter replied most generously, "I find it the most extraordinary piece of wit and wisdom that America has yet contributed. . . . I greet you at the beginning of a great career." The fact that Whitman was brash enough to print Emerson's letter in the second edition of the *Leaves* and, to Emerson's shocked embarrassment, put "I greet you at the Beginning of a Great Career—R. W. Emerson" on the cover, tells us a good deal about the difference in the two men's personalities, but does not detract from the significance of their encounter. Whitman and the Transcendentalists may have been different kinds of people, but their intellectual sympathies were profound.

The coming of the Civil War had a decisive impact on the last half of Whitman's career. How could he continue to sing "the great psalm of the republic" while the republic was flaming in ruins all about him? How could he chant of brotherhood, when brothers were locked in bloody combat across the nation?

> Year that trembled and reel'd beneath me!
> Your summer wind was warm enough, yet the air I breathed
> froze me
> A thick gloom fell through the sunshine and darken'd me,
> Must I change my triumphant songs? said I to myself,
> Must I indeed learn to chant the cold dirges of the baffled
> And sullen hymns of defeat?

It is a tribute to Whitman's integrity and to the comprehensiveness and strength of his vision that he continued to write exalted poetry about America.

Whitman's biographer Henry Seidel Canby finds that the war had a double effect on him. In the first place he realized that the American mission had been diverted and that the war was necessary to preserve it. At the same time Whitman's own experience during the war enhanced his faith in democracy. This experience was gained in the hospitals around Washington where he worked as an aide. In "Song of Myself" he had written, "I was the man, I suffered, I was there." Now he was there. In his first visit he saw a pile of amputated feet, arms, and legs under a tree in front of a camp hospital. He stayed to give comfort to the wounded, write letters to parents, wives, and sweethearts, distribute tobacco and fruit. As he sat by the bedsides of the dying young men, fanning and wiping the sweat from their faces, he was struck by their courage, endurance, and lack of complaint. They were the stuff of democracy and they became a part of Whitman's poetry after the war, a poetry in which, as Canby points out, Whitman's "amorphous" idealism "crystallized," in which there was less rhetoric, less of Whitman himself, and a calm certainty about democracy. The compassionate and controlled verses in *Drum Taps* and the matchless lyrics of "When Lilacs Last in the Dooryard Bloom'd" testify to the more serene Whitman of the latter years.

In 1876, when he was almost sixty, Whitman issued a centennial edition of *Leaves of Grass*. "I count with . . . absolute certainty in the great future of the United States," he wrote in the preface, "America, too, is a prophecy. . . . Within my time the United States have emerged from nebulous vagueness and suspense to full . . . decision—have done the deeds and achiev'd the triumphs of half a score of centuries—and are henceforth to enter upon their real history."

THE NOVEL IN AMERICA

So far as we know none of Whitman's contemporaries ever said "The United States themselves are the greatest novel." Even more than poets and painters, American novelists felt that democratic society offered scanty materials with which to work. Cooper put the problem as well as anyone when he wrote in *Notions of the Americans:* "There is scarcely an ore which contributes to the wealth of the author, that is found, here, in veins as rich as in Europe. There are no annals for the historian; no follies (beyond the most vulgar and commonplace) for the satirist; no manners for the dramatist; no obscure fictions for the writer of romance; no gross and hardy offences against decorum for the moralist; nor any of the rich artificial auxiliaries of poetry."

Cooper's sentiments were later re-echoed by Hawthorne and Henry James among others. This being the case, with so many of our major writers sensible to the difficulties involved in writing traditional novels in America, it should not surprise us to discover the American novel taking on a distinctive style. Richard Chase in his study, *The American Novel and Its Tradition,* tells us that the quality of "romance" has always been characteristic of the American novel. By this he means that the American novel has been less faithful than the British to social reality; it has emphasized action more than character, and has tied character more to ideal types than to particular social classes. Romance features extraordinary plots (as does *Moby Dick*) and there is usually a heavy reliance on symbolism and allegory.

James Fenimore Cooper may be considered the first distinctively American novelist because he embodied both the quality of romance and basic contradictory impulses within American culture in his novels. Cooper was a man of extraordinary energy, who published more than fifty books and pamphlets from 1820 to 1850, and wrote on almost every subject. By common consent his great achievement is the five *Leatherstocking Tales* which appeared sporadically between 1823 and 1841. The five novels recount the adventures of the backwoodsman Leatherstocking from about 1740 to 1806. In creating the forest novel and a character like Leatherstocking, Cooper was writing "romance." These are not realistic studies of life on the frontier, but imaginative tales featuring a character who represents both the nobility and innocence of the wilderness and the threat to civilization that the wilderness represents. Leatherstocking is an ambiguous hero who symbolizes one of the most important conflicts within the American mind at mid-century. This contradiction has been pointed out by Henry Nash Smith and a host of other historians and critics. Perry Miller states it clearly in an essay on Melville: "A clue to the national expression of this period above all others . . . was an inward dread lest the obstinate advance of culture destroy the natural simplicity of the land. At the same time, culture exerted a horrible fascination, and for lack of it the country stood condemned of provinciality and boorishness."

In creating Leatherstocking, whom Balzac called a "magnificent moral hermaphrodite born between the savage and civilized worlds," Cooper launched the American novel on its course. Two greater artists of the period, Hawthorne and Melville, were also to emphasize "romance" and the paradoxical forces of American culture.

NATHANIEL HAWTHORNE:
THE DEMOCRAT AS PURITAN

Hawthorne was a Puritan both by lineage and by temperament. Born in Salem, Massachusetts, he went to Bowdoin College and after graduation returned to Salem where he spent twelve years in his mother's house perfecting his craft as a writer. It was natural that his inspiration should have been peopled by ghosts and witches and old New England legends. His first ancestor, Major William Hawthorne, who had come to America in 1630, had been a bitter persecutor of the Quakers. Hawthorne's mind was introspective and dwelt upon the past. "Strong strains of their nature," he said, referring to the Puritans, "have intertwined themselves with mine." The writers who meant the most to him, Spenser, Milton, and Bunyan, only reinforced his natural inclinations, and the sketches, short stories, and novels that he wrote all reflect the profound influence of the Puritan past.

Hawthorne spent a good part of his later life in Concord. He went hiking with Emerson and boating with Thoreau, but he found their companionship more appealing than their philosophy. All three were children of the Puritans, but Hawthorne had not been reborn into the "new views." His most intimate and intensive experience with Transcendentalism came in 1841 when he joined the Brook Farm Community at West Roxbury, Massachusetts, a utopian experiment in communal living under the leadership of George Ripley, one of Emerson's disciples. Here he got to see rather more than he liked of Margaret Fuller, another Emerson satellite, who, he said, was "full of borrowed qualities," and to learn that utopia was not for him.

In 1843 and 1844 Hawthorne delivered his judgment on the Transcendentalists in two short sketches. The first, entitled

"The Celestial Railroad," recounts the experiences of a modern Christian pilgrim, who attempts to make his way to the heavenly city by railroad. He is accompanied by various individuals with names like Mr. Smooth-it-away, Mr. Love-for-the-world, Mr. Hide-sin-in-the-heart, and Mr. Scaly-conscience. He learns that the slough of despond, which had caused such anguish for Bunyan's earlier pilgrim, has been conveniently bridged and that the bridge is anchored in foundations concocted of "volumes of French philosophy and German rationalism . . . essays of modern clergymen" and "extracts from Plato, Confucius, and various Hindoo sages. . . ." Bunyan's two giants, Pope and Pagan, have been replaced by a Giant Transcendentalist shrouded in fog, and the enormous burden which Christian had borne on his back is now being carried in the baggage car. The train never reaches the celestial city because, as we learn at the end, the guide on the journey, Mr. Smooth-it-away, is really in league with the devil.

The point which Hawthorne makes in this simple parody is one to which he returns throughout his writing. Evil exists as a powerful and active force in the world, and man's struggle with it is bloody and everlasting. In his novel *The Marble Faun,* for example, Hawthorne has one of his characters criticize the lack of realism in Guido's painting of the victory of Archangel Michael over Lucifer.

Is it thus that virtue looks the moment after its death-struggle with evil? No, no; I could have told Guido better. A full third of the Archangel's feathers should have been torn from his wings; the rest all ruffled, till they looked like Satan's own! His sword should be streaming with blood, and perhaps broken half-way to the hilt; his armor crushed, his robes rent, his breast gory; a bleeding gash on his brow, cutting right across the stern scowl of battle! He should press his foot hard down upon the old serpent, as if his very soul depended upon it, feeling him squirm mightily, and doubting whether the fight were half over yet, and how the victory might turn! . . . The battle never was such child's play as Guido's dapper Archangel seems to have found it. ʹ

Hawthorne differed with the Transcendentalists not only in matters of religion and personal salvation, but also on social reform. His sketch "Earth's Holocaust" describes a great bonfire on the Western prairies fed by reformers who want to get rid of all the outmoded rubbish cluttering up modern democratic society. First to go into the blaze are the trappings of aristocracy, followed in close order by royal robes and crowns, all the weapons of the world, wine and tobacco, the gallows, deeds of property, marriage certificates, political constitutions, and finally the Holy Bible. "The inhabitants of the earth had grown too enlightened to define their faith within a form of words, or to limit the spiritual by any analogy to our material existence. Truths which the heavens trembled at were now but a fable of the world's infancy." At the end of the tale the narrator concludes that the reformers had burned up the world without reaching the source of human misery. "The heart, the heart,—there was the little yet boundless sphere wherein existed the original wrong of which the crime and misery of this outward world were merely types. Purify that inward sphere and the many shapes of evil that haunt the outward, and which now seem almost our only realities, will turn to shadowy phantoms and vanish of their own accord. . . ."

Hawthorne's deep sense of sin and his conviction of the reality and permanence of evil as a force in the world made him conservative in politics. He was an active Democrat and an admirer of Andrew Jackson, but did not share the perfectionist faith entertained by so many of his contemporaries. He had been a classmate of Franklin Pierce at Bowdoin, and when Pierce was nominated candidate for President by the Democrats in 1852, Hawthorne was commissioned to write the campaign biography. He defended Pierce's support of the Compromise of 1850 in language that would have done justice to Webster. Pierce, he said, was a man "who dared to love that great and sacred reality—his whole, united, native country—better than the mistiness of a philanthropic theory." The wise man, in Hawthorne's view, would look upon slavery "as one of those evils which divine Providence does not leave to be remedied by human contrivances, but which in its own good time, by means impossible to be anticipated, . . . it causes to vanish like a dream."

Another way in which Hawthorne differed from thinkers like Emerson, Thoreau, and Whitman was his concern with the dangers of individualism. He was himself a self-reliant person, and for all his faith in Providence believed that a man had to make his own way in the world. "The fault of a failure is attributable," he said, "in a great degree at least—to the man who fails. . . . Nobody has a right to live in the world unless he be strong and able, and applies his ability to good purpose." At the same time he agreed with the Puritans that pride was a cardinal sin and he recognized, as the Puritans and Transcendentalists never did, the danger of the alienated individual. In Hawthorne's work the characters who separate themselves from the rest of society on the basis of superior intellect or ideological conviction come to an unhappy end. Ethan Brand, who undertakes to discover the "unpardonable sin," by so doing commits that sin and is consumed by his own monomania. Dr. Rappaccini employs his science to make his daughter superior to ordinary women and ends up poisoning her. In like manner Hawthorne's most tortured characters are those who are alienated from others by some secret, guilty knowledge they cannot reveal. Arthur Dimmesdale is perhaps the most famous example. He has committed adultery with Hester Prynne. She has been punished, but his participation in the sin is not discovered. He retains his position as the minister and spiritual leader of the community, and his awareness of his own sin makes him an even more powerful preacher. The congregation treats him like a saint, but he thinks of himself as a monster and under the stress of this spiritual estrangement his whole personality begins to disintegrate.

For Hawthorne, partly because of his own solitary vigil as an apprentice writer, partly because of his intense awareness of the common plight of mankind, the things that unite people are more precious than the things that separate them. The human heart may be a source of evil, but it is also a source of love. Those of Hawthorne's characters who deny the affectional impulses in themselves are transformed into fiends. Ethan Brand, for example, allows an intellectual obsession with the "unpardonable sin" to destroy his humanity.

He remembered with what tenderness, with what love and sympathy for mankind, and what pity for human guilt and woe, he had first begun to contemplate those ideas which afterwards became the inspiration of his life, with what reverence he had then looked into the heart of man, viewing it as a temple originally divine, and however desecrated, still to be held sacred by a brother. . . . Then ensued that vast intellectual development, which in its progress disturbed the counterpoise between his mind and heart . . . that indeed had withered—had contracted—had hardened—had perished! It had ceased to partake of the universal throb. He had lost his hold of the magnetic charm of humanity.

It will not do to dismiss Hawthorne as a pessimist. That he was a child of the Puritans inclined to see the darker aspects of life is true. That he felt there could be no wisdom without a knowledge of evil is also true. Still Hawthorne's world is one of light as well as shadow. He is expressing the Puritan mind of nineteenth century American democracy. His belief in the sanctity of the human heart and the natural ties of human sympathy have more in common with Channing than with Jonathan Edwards.

HERMAN MELVILLE:
THE DEMOCRAT AS SKEPTIC

What journalism was to Whitman and Salem was to Hawthorne the sea was to Herman Melville. He once said a whaling ship was "my Yale College and my Harvard." Melville was born in New York City in 1819. His family moved to Albany where Melville's father died in 1832 deeply in debt. Herman tried his hand at schoolteaching and shipped out to sea for the first time when he was twenty years old. In 1841 he signed on to the whaler *Acushnet* out of New Bedford, Massachusetts. Three years later, after jumping ship in the South Pacific to get away from a tyrannical captain, and living for a while with friendly cannibals, he docked at Boston and began his career as a writer. His experiences at sea provided him with the materials for five novels which appeared in rapid succession, *Typee* 1846, *Omoo* 1847, *Mardi* 1849, *Redburn* 1849, *White-Jacket* 1850. His masterpiece, *Moby Dick,* was published in 1851.

Melville's career as a writer extended almost to the end of the century. He died in relative obscurity in 1891, and *Billy Budd,* the short novel he was working on at his death, was not published until 1924. For our understanding of Melville as a representative of the American mind at mid-century, however, *Moby Dick* is the key book.

Most critics would agree that *Moby Dick* is the greatest American novel; some would call it the greatest in the English language. Like most great novels it is at once simple and complex and can be read on several levels at the same time. Rich in symbolism, it is a critic's delight and hundreds of books and articles have been written attempting to explain it. The basic story is familiar to most educated Americans. A young, introspective seaman, Ishmael (the narrator) joins the crew of the whaler *Pequod* in Nantucket under Captain Ahab. After setting out to sea Ahab announces that the purpose of the voyage is to search out and kill Moby Dick, the legendary white whale who in a previous voyage had sheared off his leg. The novel recounts the hunt for Moby Dick and ends when the great whale destroys the *Pequod* and all the crew save Ishmael. This is the novel on the simplest posible level. On another level it is a profound criticism of American values and a searching inquiry into the problem of good and evil and the nature of the universe.

Many observers have noticed the strongly American qualities in Melville's book. In his study of Melville's thought entitled *The Tragedy of Mind,* William Ellery Sedgwick claims that Melville achieves some of his extraordinary effects by "adding Hawthorne's human interiors to Thoreau's nature." He might have added "with Whitman's expansiveness," for Melville is at home in the great open spaces of the sea as well as in the secret places of the heart. The shaggy, ferocious Ahab is an American figure. Melville likens him to the last of the grizzly bears living near settlements in the West, and his single-minded pursuit of the whale has its counterpart in the pioneer's confrontation of the wilderness and the Puritan's solitary quest for salvation.

Along with its American flavor *Moby Dick* carries a biting indictment of American values. If we take the whaling industry as symbolic of the success of American enterprise, then Ahab becomes a prototype for the strong-minded, ruthless tycoon who will play such an important role in despoiling American resources and building up American industry in the last half of the nineteenth century. "Swerve me?" Ahab asks, "the path to my fixed purpose is laid with iron rails, whereon my soul is grooved to run. Over unsounded gorges, through the rifled hearts of mountains, under torrents' beds, unerringly I rush! Naught's an obstacle, naught's an angle to the iron way!" To the extent that Melville repudiates Ahab, we can say that he is repudiating the materialistic emphasis of American individualism.

If the novel is a criticism of American materialism, so is it also of American idealism. Melville was friendly with Hawthorne and said he liked the "blackness" in the latter's work. He shared Hawthorne's reservations about the wisdom of the Transcendentalists. "I do not oscillate in Emerson's rainbow," he wrote a friend two years before *Moby Dick* was published, "but prefer to hang myself in mine own halter than swing in any other man's swing." He apparently thought of Emerson as an armchair philosopher, taking his ease in Concord while declaiming on the benevolence of nature and the divinity of man. Melville had seen men flogged at sea and had lived with cannibals. "To one who has weathered Cape Horn," he wrote in the margin of a volume of Emerson's essays, "what stuff all this is." In another place, he wrote that Emerson's "gross and astounding errors and illusions spring from a self-conceit so intensely intellectual and calm that at first one hesitates to call it by its right name." As Melville describes Ahab, it is easy to visualize him as Emerson's transcendental, self-reliant man drawing all his inspiration from nature and within himself: ". . . a man of greatly superior natural force, with a globular brain and a ponderous heart; who has also by the stillness and seclusion of many long night-watches in the remotest waters, and beneath constellations never seen at the north, been led to think untraditionally and independently; receiving all nature's sweet or savage impressions fresh from her own virgin voluntary and confiding breast." Emerson once said that if he were the devil's son he would live from the devil. Thoreau said that no man ever followed his genius until it misled him. To the extent that Ahab seems to be the incarnation of such ideas we can say that *Moby Dick* is a product of Melville's disgust with Transcendentalism.

Yet, as Perry Miller points out in his essay *Melville and Transcendentalism,* the novel cannot be comprehended in these terms alone. Ahab is not a villain but a tragic hero. His madness springs originally from his nobility, for it is noble to search for truth and to conquer evil. To the extent that the whale represents evil and to the extent that Ahab, even on the brink of his own destruction, refuses to admit defeat, there is a grandeur to his character. In almost his last breath Ahab calls Moby Dick "thou all-destroying but unconquering whale." Ahab's body is destroyed; his spirit remains defiant, and in this sense he is a transcendental hero.

The same year that *Moby Dick* was published Melville read Hawthorne's "Ethan Brand." Hawthorne's character has much in common with Ahab, and Melville wrote to Hawthorne saying, "I stand for the heart. To the dogs with the head! I had rather be a fool with a heart, than Jupiter Olympus with his head." Melville's criticism of Ahab seems to be the same as Hawthorne's criticism of Ethan Brand. Ahab's search for the whale, like the search for the unpardonable sin, becomes an obsession. Self-reliance is transformed into monomania. The result is not only destruction for all around him, but spiritual anguish and isolation within himself. "This lovely light," Ahab mutters, "it lights not me; all loveliness is anguish to me, since I can ne'er enjoy. Gifted with the high perception, I lack the low enjoying power; damned, most subtly and most malignantly."

In 1856 Melville visited Hawthorne in England. Hawthorne's report of the meeting helps to explain the difference between the two men.

Melville, as he always does, began to reason of Providence, and futurity, and of everything that lies beyond human ken, and informed me that he had "pretty much made up his mind to be annihilated"; but still he does not seem to rest in that anticipation; and, I think, will never rest until he gets hold of a definite belief.

It is strange how he persists and has persisted ever since I knew him, and probably long before—in wandering to and fro over these deserts. . . . He can neither believe, nor be comfortable in his unbelief; and he is too honest and courageous not to try to do one or the other.

In a society of believers Melville was a skeptic who wanted to believe, but he could not share Hawthorne's faith in Providence. For Melville the moral ambiguity of the universe was the last reality. Ahab is full of contradictory qualities. His courage and indomitable will are matched by his ruthlessness to others and an obsession which makes him project his own evil on to the whale. Good and evil, himself, Ahab is a symbol of the moral ambiguity in man and nature. Melville asks us to consider "the universal cannibalism of the sea . . . and then turn to the green, gentle, and most docile earth; consider them both . . . and do you not find a strange analogy to something in yourself?"

When Ahab and his crew plunge to their grave, only Moby Dick and Ishmael survive. The whale, interpreted by various critics to represent evil, God, or the inscrutable power of nature, swims away, and Ishmael remains afloat on a coffin. Despite the symbolism he is not reborn; like Melville he remains a spiritual orphan, and his pilgrimage will never be completed.

It is appropriate that Melville should have found more readers in the twentieth century than in his own time. His skepticism and inability to reconcile the moral ambiguities in life have more meaning for us in the nuclear age than they did for the men and women of nineteenth century American democracy.

SIX

Conclusion

American thought during the middle of the nineteenth century took two major forms of expression. The first was the elaboration of a democratic faith celebrating individualism, moral law, and the American mission. The articles of the democratic faith reinforced each other and provided American theologians, philosophers, scientists, political thinkers, and artists with a common set of assumptions about themselves, the universe, and the society in which they lived.

The liberal transformation of Calvinism and the formulation of Transcendentalism were based on belief in the free individual. The same belief provided a rationale for the democratization of politics, and helped to sustain the agitation of a reformer like Wendell Phillips, as well as the more conservative philosophy of Lincoln. It helps to explain why Americans supported the achievements of practical science during the period. Scientific progress was not only an evidence of the rationality and dignity of man, but properly applied it would emancipate the laborer and make the self-fulfillment of the common man more possible. Whitman's poetry glorified the free individual, and Hawthorne and Melville wrestled with the implications of individualism in their most serious work.

Except for a rare skeptic like Melville, the most significant American thinkers in the middle of the nineteeth century were all "religious." No matter how eccentric their theology, they all found common ground in the assumption that the universe was permeated with moral law and purpose. That a philosopher or scientist might ever be brought to question this assumption would have been unthinkable to them.

Belief in the American mission was as pervasive as the belief in individualism and moral law. The symbolism the American people attached to Andrew Jackson expressed this belief. When Americans looked at Jackson they saw themselves stronger and more virtuous than Europeans because they were closer to nature, able to accomplish great things through self-reliance, comforted by the knowledge that God was on their side. Belief in the American mission, like belief in the free individual, inspired both reformers and conservatives during the period, and a fascination with the vision of America's future was a common concern of our most talented writers.

Only among Southern writers was there any serious attempt made to quarrel with the democratic faith. Although the dominant mood was more pessimistic, even here the belief in moral law and an intense individualism (among the "peerage of white men") were powerful. Some Southern intellectuals went so far as to justify slavery in terms of the democratic faith, which made white people more equal, they said, by relegating servile labor to Negroes. Southern thinkers differed most from their contemporaries in the rest of the country in their unwillingness to tolerate criticism of their own social institutions and their inability to accept the perfectionist overtones of the American mission. Even so, leading spokesmen like Calhoun and Fitzhugh found it impossible to completely disengage themselves from the dominant American faith. Calhoun's constitutionalism was imbued with the spirit of Locke and intended to protect the property rights of individuals. Fitzhugh's indictment of capitalism often sounded as humanitarian as that of any Northern reformer. To the extent that they compromised with the democratic faith, the Southerners weakened their own argument. To the extent that they rejected it, they cut themselves off from the mainstream of American thought and were ignored.

The elaboration of a democratic faith was the major concern of American political philosophers and social critics at mid-century. A liberal consensus did exist, and the only real heretics were the Southern intellectuals who defended slavery. At the same time, there was room enough within the consensus for meaningful distinctions to be made between individual thinkers. All of the most articulate voices outside the South spoke for the values of American democracy, but some of them belonged to democratic radicals who sought to make the American condition conform immediately to the idealism of the democratic faith, while others belonged to democratic conservatives, unwilling to jeopardize the achievements of American society on the basis of abstract notions of truth and justice.

The second major form of expression taken by American thought during this period can be seen in the ambivalent response that many sensitive Americans made to the tremendous changes taking place in nineteenth century American society. Recent studies have shown that the Jacksonians themselves participated in this ambivalence, on the one hand, as reformers, seeking to create conditions in which a new democratic capitalism would thrive, on the other hand, as traditionalists, frightened by the spread of business enterprise and the growth of cities, longing for the pastoral simplicity of Jefferson's America. Many of the most popular literary heroes of the period, like Cooper's Leatherstocking, symbolized the ambiguous response Americans felt as they watched in dread and fascination the march of civilization against the wilderness. As a hero of the wilderness Leatherstocking **represented** innocence, nobility, and strength.

As the enemy of civilization he represented barbarism and a threat to progress. In the work of America's most imaginative writers, like Hawthorne and Melville, it was not so much the unities but the discontinuities and contradictions within American culture that were dramatized. How, for example, could a belief in the unlimited power of the free individual be reconciled with a belief in moral law and Providence? How could the American mission be accomplished, and American society be perfected, in a nation where individual self-interest held sway? These were the kinds of questions taking up the American imagination at mid-century; Americans have been pondering them ever since.

Bibliographical Essay

CHAPTER ONE

Vernon Parrington's *The Romantic Revolution in America* which is volume two of *Main Currents in American Thought* (1927-1930) is the classic interpretation of this period from the Jeffersonian point of view. Merle Curti's *The Growth of American Thought* (1943) is the most comprehensive history of American ideas and emphasizes the triumph of democracy and nationalism during the period. Stow Persons' *American Minds* (1958) is a more analytical history and concentrates on broad concepts rather than individual thinkers. The first part of Ralph Gabriel's *The Course of American Democratic Thought* (2d edition 1956) is a brilliant discussion of unifying themes in the American mind at mid-century. Louis Hartz's *The Liberal Tradition in America* (1955) is a difficult but stimulating study which emphasizes the importance of a liberal consensus in American thought, and is especially effective in dealing with the South. Hartz's thesis may be read in summary form in an essay included in *Paths of American Thought* (1963), edited by Arthur Schlesinger, Jr., and Morton White. Alexis de Tocqueville's *Democracy in America* (1835-1840) is a basic source for all aspects of the period.

CHAPTER TWO

Two important studies of American religious thought between Edwards's time and Channing's are Joseph Haroutunian, *Piety Versus Moralism* (1932), and Sydney Mead, *Nathaniel William Taylor* (1942). David P. Edgell's *William Ellery Channing: An Intellectual Portrait* (1955) is the best critical study of Channing's ideas. William McLoughlin's *Modern Revivalism: Charles Grandison Finney to Billy Graham* (1958) is especially good on Finney. An excellent primary source for the whole period is Lyman Beecher's *Autobiography* (1961), now available in a modern edition edited by Barbara Cross who has also written the best recent study of Bushnell, *Horace Bushnell: Minister to a Changing America* (1958). Wilson Smith's *Professors and Public Ethics: Studies of Northern Moral Philosophers Before the Civil War* (1956) is a good introduction to the academic mind of the period. George Schmidt's *The Liberal Arts College: A Chapter in American Cultural History* (1957) is also valuable. The literature on Emerson and Transcendentalism is enormous. Perry Miller's introduction to *The Transcendentalists: An Anthology* (1950) is excellent, but no one has really improved on the accounts of Transcendentalism that Emerson and Theodore Parker wrote themselves. These essays "Theodore Parker's Experience as a Minister" and "Historic Notes of Life and Letters in New England" are included in the Miller anthology. Two valuable recent studies of Emerson's thought are Sherman Paul, *Emerson's Angle of Vision* (1952), and Stephen Whicher, *Freedom and Fate* (1953).

There is no inclusive study of American science in the first half of the nineteenth century comparable to Brooke Hindle's *The Pursuit of Science in Revolutionary America* (1956). Dirk Struik's *Yankee Science in the Making* (1948) covers New England. Hunter Dupree's *Science in the Federal Government, A History of Policies and Activities to 1940* (1957) is good for this period. John Oliver's *History of American Technology* (1956) is a useful descriptive account of technology during the period, and Siegfried Giedion's *Mechanization Takes Command* (1948) is a brilliant attempt to relate technological development to the American mind. Edward Lurie's *Louis Agassiz: A Life in Science* (1960) and Hunter Dupree's *Asa Gray 1810-1888* (1959) are two recent biographies that illuminate the American scientific mind before Darwin. Donald

Fleming's "American Science and the World Scientific Community" (*Journal of World History* 1965) is an insightful essay which helps to explain the distinguishing characteristics of American science during the period.

CHAPTER THREE

The clearest summary of the historiography of the Jacksonian period is Charles Sellers's *Jacksonian Democracy* (1958), published by the Service Center for Teachers of History. The two best recent studies of the intellectual history of the period are Marvin Meyers's *The Jacksonian Persuasion* (1957), which emphasizes the ambivalence in Jacksonian thought toward change, and John W. Ward's *Andrew Jackson: Symbol for an Age* (1953), which points up the symbolic qualities of Jackson for the American mind. Lee Benson's *The Concept of Jacksonian Democracy* (1961) emphasizes the egalitarianism of the period and questions the use of "Jacksonianism" as a unifying theme. Richard Hofstadter's "William Leggett, Spokesman of Jacksonian Democracy," *Political Science Quarterly* (December, 1943), is excellent, as is Russell Nye's biography, *George Bancroft: Brahmin Rebel* (1944).

The most recent comprehensive study of the reform movements in the period is Louis Filler's *The Crusade Against Slavery, 1830-1860* (1960). Alice Felt Tyler's *Freedom's Ferment* (1944) and Gilbert Barnes's *The Anti-Slavery Impulse* (1933) emphasize the importance of religion to reform. Walter Roy Harding, *A Thoreau Handbook* (1959), is a good introduction to Thoreau's ideas. Leo Stoller's *After Walden: Thoreau's Changing Views on Economic Man* (1957) is a provocative study of Thoreau's social philosophy. Sherman Paul's *The Shores of America* (1958) is the most recent and comprehensive study of Thoreau's ideas. For recent interpretations of the abolitionists see Martin Duberman (editor), *The Antislavery Vanguard: New Essays on the Abolitionists* (1965), John L. Thomas's *The Liberator: William Lloyd Garrison* (1963), and Irving H. Bartlett's *Wendell Phillips: Brahmin Radical* (1961).

Clinton Rossiter's *Conservatism in America* (1955) is the best book on the subject. Richard Current's *Daniel Webster and the Rise of National Conservatism* (1955) emphasizes the qualities in Webster's thinking that Rossiter finds common to American conservatism. Despite the enormous literature on Lincoln the best guide to the quality of his mind is found in his own writing, in David

Donald's *Lincoln Reconsidered* (1956), in Richard Hofstadter's essay on Lincoln in *The American Political Tradition* (1948), and in the essays edited by Norman Graebner, *The Enduring Lincoln* (1959). T. Harry Williams's *Abraham Lincoln: Selected Speeches, Messages and Letters* (1957) is a useful one-volume edition of Lincoln's writing with a good introductory essay on Lincoln's thought. William J. Wolf's *The Almost Chosen People* (1959) is the best study of Lincoln's religous ideas. Lincoln's conservatism can be studied in T. Harry Williams's *Lincoln and the Radicals* and in chapters fourteen and fifteen of Irving H. Bartlett's *Wendell Phillips: Brahmin Radical* (1961).

CHAPTER FOUR

Wilbur Cash's *The Mind of the South* (1941) is a brilliantly written study which emphasizes both the democratic and nondemocratic qualities in the Southern mind. The book deals with the Southern mind collectively rather than with individual thinkers. Its chief flaw is an absence of documentation. Clement Eaton's *The Growth of Southern Civilization* (1961) is the most complete study of its kind. Eaton's *The Mind of the Old South* (1964) is a collection of intellectual portraits of representative Southern thinkers. John Hope Franklin's *The Militant South 1800-1861* (1956) is the authoritative study of the subject. William Stanton's *The Leopard's Spots: Scientific Attitudes Toward Race in America, 1815-59* (1960) is a valuable study of the South's contribution to scientific thought. Eric McKitrick's *Slavery Defended: The Views of the Old South* (1963) is a good anthology of proslavery thought. The most comprehensive study of Calhoun is Charles Wiltse's three-volume biography. Calhoun's ideas are sharply delineated in Richard Hofstadter's *The American Political Tradition* (1948), and in Richard Current's "John C. Calhoun, Philosopher of Reaction," *Antioch Review* (Summer, 1943), and Margaret L. Coit's *John C. Calhoun: An American Portrait* (1950). Stanley Elkins, *Slavery: A Problem in American Institutional and Intellectual Life* (1959), is a brilliant analysis of slavery and the quality of the American mind that attacked and supported it. Kenneth Stampp's *The Peculiar Institution: Slavery in the Ante-Bellum South* (1956) is an authoritative study and should be read in conjunction with Elkins. C. Vann Woodward's introduction to a new edition of *Cannibals All* (1960) is a concise analysis of Fitzhugh's ideas. Harvey Wish, *George Fitzhugh: Propagandist for the Old South* (1943), is the standard biography. William R. Taylor's *Cavalier and Yankee: The Old South and American National Character* (1961) is an important study showing how the myth of the South helped to allay deep-seated anxieties in the American mind regarding the pace of change and the materialism of the period.

CHAPTER FIVE

Benjamin Spencer's *The Quest for Nationality* (1957) is authoritative on the efforts of Americans to develop a national literature. F. O. Matthiessen's *American Renaissance* (1941) is still the classic study of America's foremost writers. The subtitle *Art and Expression in the Age of Emerson and Whitman* suggests the author's emphasis. The first volume of the *Literary History of the United States* (1948) covers the writers of the mid-century and incorporates most recent interpretations up to 1948. Significant recent studies in the mythical qualities of American literature during the period are Henry Nash Smith, *Virgin Land* (1950), which treats the myth of the West in American popular literature, R. W. B. Lewis, *The American Adam* (1955), which traces themes of innocence, tragedy, and tradition through the classic writers, and Charles Sanford, *The Quest for Paradise* (1961), which develops the myth of Eden in the American imagination. Richard Chase's essay "The Classic Literature: Art and Idea," in *Paths of American Thought* (1963) is a good analysis of the impact of modern literary criticism on our conception of the major writers in the period. His *The American Novel and Its Tradition* (1957) is a stimulating attempt to show that the distinctively American quality of mind creates a distinctively American form in fiction. Of course no amount of literary criticism can replace the works of the great writers themselves. Whitman's *Leaves of Grass* can be usefully supplemented with Henry Seidel Canby's *Walt Whitman* (1943), which has an interesting account of Whitman's relationship to Emerson and Thoreau, and with *Whitman: A Collection of Critical Essays* (1962), edited by Roy Pearce. The two clearest statements of Hawthorne's thought outside his own stories and novels are in the final chapter of Randall Stewart's *Nathaniel Hawthorne, A Biography* (1948) and Austin Warren's introduction to *Nathaniel Hawthorne* (1934), in the American Writers Series. William Ellery Sedgwick's *Herman Mel-*

ville, The Tragedy of Mind (1944) is the best study of Melville's thought. *Moby-Dick Centennial Essays* (1953), edited by Tyrus Hillway and Luther Mansfield, is an interesting collection and includes important essays by Perry Miller and Randall Stewart on the interrelationships among Emerson, Hawthorne, and Melville.

INDEX

Calhoun, John C. (*cont.*)
  for secession, 63
  on slavery, 83
Calvinism, 23, 81
  transformation of, 7-18, 114
Cambridge Observatory, 31
Canby, Henry Seidel, 102
Cannibals All! or Slaves Without Masters (Fitzhugh), 87-88
capitalism, 61, 68-69, 83, 87-88, 116
  development of, 2-3
  Jacksonian concept of, 36-37
Carman, Harry, 66
Cash, Wilbur, 74
Cavalier and Yankee (Taylor), 2, 76
"cavalier" image, 75-76
"Celestial Railroad, The" (Hawthorne), 106
change, attitudes toward, 2, 4, 17-18, 44-45, 57-58, 76, 90, 116-117
Channing, William Ellery, 8-13, 21
  on Calvinism, 10-11
  on God, 10
  on rationalism, 10
Charleston, S.C., 78
Chase, Richard, 104, *quoted* 97
Chauncy, Charles, 9, 22
cholera epidemics, 31
Christian Nurture (Bushnell), 15-16
civil disobedience, 46-48
"Civil Disobedience" (Thoreau), 43, 45-46
Civilization in the United States (Stearns), 6
Civil War, 67, 102
Clay, Henry, 58, 63
Coit, Margaret, 82
Coleridge, Samuel Taylor, 14-17, 22
colleges, 18-20, 74
Colt, Samuel, 26
Compromise of 1850, 64, 107

"concurrent majority," 85-86
Congregationalists, 9, 41
conservatism
  of academic philosophers, 20
  democratic, 33, 64-65, 116
  of Hawthorne, 107
  Jacksonian, 33-34, 37
  within liberal tradition, 55-56
  and majority rule, 57, 60
  national, 60-64
  organicism of, 90
  principles of (Rossiter), 56
  problems of, 59
  and reform, 42
  and religion, 59
  in South, 80, 83, 115-116
Conservatism in America (Rossiter), 56
Constitution, 71, 82
constitutionalism, 56-57, 60, 65, 71, 84, 116
Cooper, James Fenimore, 94, 104-105, 116
  on paucity of material in U.S., 103
cotton mills, 55
Cousin, Victor, 15
Crandall, Prudence, 50
Cross, Barbara, 18
Current, Richard, 60

Darwin, Charles, 31
Declaration of Independence, 33, 39, 70-71, 83, 89
Deism, 8-9
Democrats, 58-59, 98-99
  Jacksonian, 3, 33-38, 116
Dew, Thomas R., *quoted* 79
Disquisition on Government (Calhoun), 84
Donald, David, 41
Dorr, Thomas, 60
Douglas, Stephen, 66, 69
Dresser, Amos, 50
Drum Taps (Whitman), 103

"Earth's Holocaust" (Hawthorne), *quoted* 107
Eaton, Clement, *quoted* 78
economics, 33-37
education, 18-20, 74, 77
Edwards, Jonathan, 7-13, 21-22, 24
Elements of Moral Science (Wayland), 19
Elkins, Stanley, 41-42, 49, *quoted* 42
Emerson, Ralph Waldo, 20-25, 40, 77, 95-97, 100-102
  on American intellectualism, 95
  on intuition, 23-24
  on *Leaves of Grass*, 102
  Melville's opinion of, 111
  on poetry, 101
  on reason, 23
  on Theodore Parker, 11
  on Thoreau, 44
  on Transcendentalism, 22-23
Emerson's Angle of Vision (Paul), 24
Enlightenment, 3, 23
  in American religious thought, 7-12
  influence on philosophical thought, 20
  "Reactionary," in South, 80
equality, 2, 32, 39
  criticisms of, 87-90
  Jacksonian concept of, 36-37
  racial, 69, 74-75, 79
  in South, 74, 115
"Ethan Brand" (Hawthorne), 108-109, 112, *quoted* 109
exploration, 30
Exposition and Protest (Calhoun), 81-82

Federalist Paper Number 10 (Madison), 76, 85
Federalists, 57-59
Filmer, Robert, Sir, 91-92

Finney, Charles Grandison, 8-14, 40
Fitzhugh, George, 68, 80, 86-93, 116
  on capitalism, 87, 88
  on equality, 87
  on institutions, 90
  on slavery, 89-91, 93
  on socialism, 88-89
Fleming, Donald, *quoted* 26, 27
Force Bill, 82
Franklin, Benjamin, 7-9, 23
Franklin, John Hope, 77
Freedom and Fate (Whicher), 24
Freedom's Ferment (Tyler), 39
frontier
  as decisive influence in shaping America, 2-4
  effect of, on South, 74
  impact of, on Lincoln, 65
  in literature, 104
  myth of, 40-41
  religion on, 12
  as symbol, 69
Frontier Mind, The (Moore), 2
Fuller, Margaret, 105

Gabriel, Ralph, 1
Gardner, Henry, 52-53
Garrison, William Lloyd, 40, 48-50
Genius of American Politics, The (Boorstin), 33
geologic surveys, 30
Gidieon, Siegfried, *quoted* 28-29
Girard, Stephen, 59
Gliddon, George, 75
God in Christ (Bushnell), 15-17
Goodyear, Charles, 26
Graebner, Norman, *quoted* 64
Gray, Asa, 29
Great Awakening, 9, 12, 14, 22
Growth of American Democratic Thought, The (Gabriel), 1

Harrison, William Henry, 58
Hartz, Louis, 3, *quoted* 32, 92
Hathorne, William, 105
Hawthorne, Nathaniel, 2, 96-97,
    103, 105-109, 111, 115, 117
  critical concern with religious
    ideas of, 6
  on evil, 106
  on humanity, 109
  on individualism, 108
  judgment of Transcendentalists,
    106
  on Melville, 112-113
  on Pierce, 107
  on Puritanism, 105
  on reform, 107
  on slavery, 107-108
Henry, Joseph, 26, 29-30
Hindle, Brooke, *quoted* 25
History of the United States (Ban-
    croft), 37
Hoe, Richard, 26
Holmes, George Frederick, *quoted*
    79-80
Holmes, Oliver Wendell, *quoted*
    28, 95
*Horace Bushnell: Minister to a
    Changing America* (Cross),
    17-18
Howe, Elias, 26
Hume, David, 19, 24
Hutchinson, Anne, 21

idealism, 22-23
ideology, 2-3
individualism, 2-4, 25, 32, 114-117
  danger of loss of, 51
  Hawthorne's view of, 108
  Melville's views on, 111
  in reform movements, 42
  in South, 74
industrialization, 45, 55, 57-58, 61,
    116
Irving, Washington, 94-95

Jackson, Andrew, 33-36, 38, 65, 76,
    82, 115
  on national bank, 34
  opposed to reform movements,
    39
  on public will, 35
  on rotation in office, 11
Jacksonian Persuasion, The (Mey-
    ers), 33
James, Henry, 104
Jefferson, Thomas, 39, 89-91,
    quoted 46

Kant, Immanuel, 22
Kennedy, John Pendleton, 76
Kent, Chancellor, 56
Kentucky, 2-3, 12, 78

labor, 35, 55, 68-69, 83, 87-89, 115
language, 16-17
Leatherstocking Tales (Cooper),
    104, 116-117
Leaves of Grass (Whitman), 99-
    103
Lectures on Revivals (Finney), 13
Leggett, William, 36-37, *quoted* 35
Leopard's Spots, The (Stanton),
    75
Lewis, R. W. B., *quoted* 41
"liberal consensus," 3, 32-33, 64,
    116
liberalism, 2-3, 36-37, 56; *see also*
    reform
Liberal Tradition in America, The
    (Hartz), 3, 92
Lincoln, Abraham, 33, 53, 64-72,
    76, 115
  on American mission, 70, 72
  on constitutional interpretation,
    71
  on erosion of American values,
    71
  on extension of slavery, 68, 69
  on free labor, 68, 69
  on government, 65

religion (*cont.*)

    in conservative tradition, 56, 59-60, 65

    and democratic tradition, 7

    history of, renewed interest in, 6

    and justification of slavery, 78-79

    Lincoln's views on, 66-68

    periods of revival in, 12

    and philosophy, 18-25

    as a primary concern of American mind, 6-7

    and reform, 38-40, 48-49

    and science, 14, 29, 31

    in South, 75

    see also individual denominations

Review of the Debate in the Virginia Legislature (Dew), 79

revivalism, 8, 75

Revolution, 61, 90

Rhode Island, 60

Ripley, George, 105

romanticism, 9, 22, 104

Rosenberg, Charles, *quoted* 31

Rossiter, Clinton, 56

Ruffin, Edmund, 75

Sanford, Charles L., *quoted* 41

Schleiermacher, Friedrich, 15

science

    government support of, 30-31

    natural, 27

    practical, 25-29, 115

    pure, 26, 30-31

    relation to philosophy, 18

    and religion, 14, 29, 31

    in South, 75

    specialization in, 29-30

secession, 71, 82, 86

Sedgwick, William Ellery, *quoted* 110

Shryock, Richard, *quoted* 28

Silliman, Benjamin, 27, 29

slavery

    extension of, 41, 62-64, 68-69

slavery (*cont.*)

    lack of criticism of, in South, 76-78

    Northern attitudes toward, 49-50, 52-53, 63, 85-86, 107-108

    Southern justifications of, 68, 75, 78-80, 82-83, 89-91, 115

Smith, Henry Nash, 40, 104

Smithsonian Institution, 30

socialism, 88-89

Sociology for the South, or the Failure of Free Society (Fitzhugh), 87

"Song of Myself" (Whitman), *quoted* 100-102

South

    cavalier image in, 75-76

    conservatism in, 80, 83, 115-116

    criticism of slavery in, stifled, 76-78

    equality in, 74, 115

    and extension of slavery, 63

    growth of, compared to North, 81

    individualism in, 74

    justification of slavery in, 68, 75, 78-80, 82-83, 89-91, 115

    majority rule in, 76-77

    militancy in, 77-78, 86

    patriarchy in, 91

    pessimism of, 77, 115

    "Reactionary Enlightenment," 80

    religion in, 75

    science in, 75

South Carolina, 81-82

Southern Literary Messenger, 79

Spencer, Benjamin, *quoted* 96

Stanton, William, 75

states' rights, 81-82, 90

Stearns, Harold, 6

Stewart, Dugald, 14, 19

Stoller, Leo, *quoted* 45, 48

Story, Justice, 56

Stringfellow, Thornton, 78

suffrage, 35-36, 56, 60, 84

HIEBERT LIBRARY

3 6877 00113 8071